GOD PRINTS

Bible FUNSTUFF

Every Season Kid Pleasin'

CHILDREN'S SERMONS

Edited By Susan Martins Miller

Foreword by
Lois Keffer

First printing 2002
1 2 3 4 5 6 7 8 9 10   07 06 05 04 03 02
Printed in the United States of America

Edited by: Susan Martins Miller

Written by: Mary Grace Becker, Sharon Bryant, Paula Frost, Dana Hood, Lois Keffer,
Janet Lee, Beth Pippin, Jennifer Root Wilger

Art Direction by Mike Riester
Cover Design by Peter Schmidt and Scot McDonald, Granite Design
Interior Design by Dana Sherrer, iDesignEtc.

Unless otherwise noted, Scripture quotations are taken from the Holy Bible:
New International Readers' Version®. Copyright © 1998 by International Bible Society.
Used by permission of Zondervan Publishing House. All rights reserved.

ISBN: 0-78143-839-X

Table of Contents

Foreword

Little feet swinging freely under the pew. Wiggly fingers looking for something to do. Eyes casting around the room in search of something to explore. Squirming children who want to see and feel and touch and move. Time for a children's sermon!

This book is full of things for swinging feet and wiggling fingers to do. You'll find fresh, interactive ways for children to see and feel and touch and move. Every sermon engages multiple senses as the kids actively participate. And that's exactly what you want them to do, because that's how they learn. Carve an apple, toss a beanbag, lick a sucker, dress up a superhero, load a backpack with rocks, fish with chocolate, tie rope knots, make "heavy metal" praise—your kids can do all these things while learning important truths about God in quick and easy children's sermons. With a few ordinary items you have around the house, you can capture the interest of curious children.

As you flip through the book, you'll find four major sections—one for each season of the year. The topics to explore and the props to gather in each section are appropriate to that season, which helps make concrete connections to the lives of kids and what they're experiencing day-to-day. You'll also find ideas for special occasions that happen seasonally, such as Back-to-School, Grandparents' Day, Thanksgiving, Christmas, Mother's Day, Father's Day, patriotic days and more.

You'll find the sermons organized in an easy way: On Your Mark, Get Set, Go!

On Your Mark!

Each children's sermon has a key Bible Verse, a Bible Truth and a Godprint. What's a Godprint? It's the touch of God on your kids. These children's sermons will help kids learn to know God and to be more like him. You're building godly character!

Get Set!

Here you'll find a list of simple items to gather—ordinary things that you're likely to have around the house or your church. In some cases, you'll also find simple set-up instructions that will make your sermon presentation go more smoothly.

Go!

Here is the "meat" of the sermon. When you see bold print, you're seeing words that you speak to the kids. If you're comfortable putting these concepts in your own words, go ahead! Other sections are explanatory or instructional. Some of the sermons have ideas for including the entire congregation. After all, even though you're speaking to a group of kids, everyone is listening in!

Here are a few simple ideas to make the most of a children's sermon:

• If the kids are on the floor, try getting on the floor yourself. Get down where you can see their faces and they can see yours.
• Use a *New International Readers' Version* of the Bible so kids can comfortably help out with reading Bible verses.
• Speak up so everyone can hear you, even the adults in the back row.
• If you ask a question, take the time to listen to answers. As much as possible, find something positive to comment on in every answer.
• Some kids are sensitive about being in front of a group. If you need special participants for the sermon you're using, choose them in a way that makes all the kids comfortable.
• Be silly! Use your voice in exaggerated ways. It gets attention!
• Remember to learn right along with the kids. Open your own heart to the insight God has for you in each sermon.

So get on your mark, get set and go! Make your few minutes with the children in your congregation memorable for the whole church.

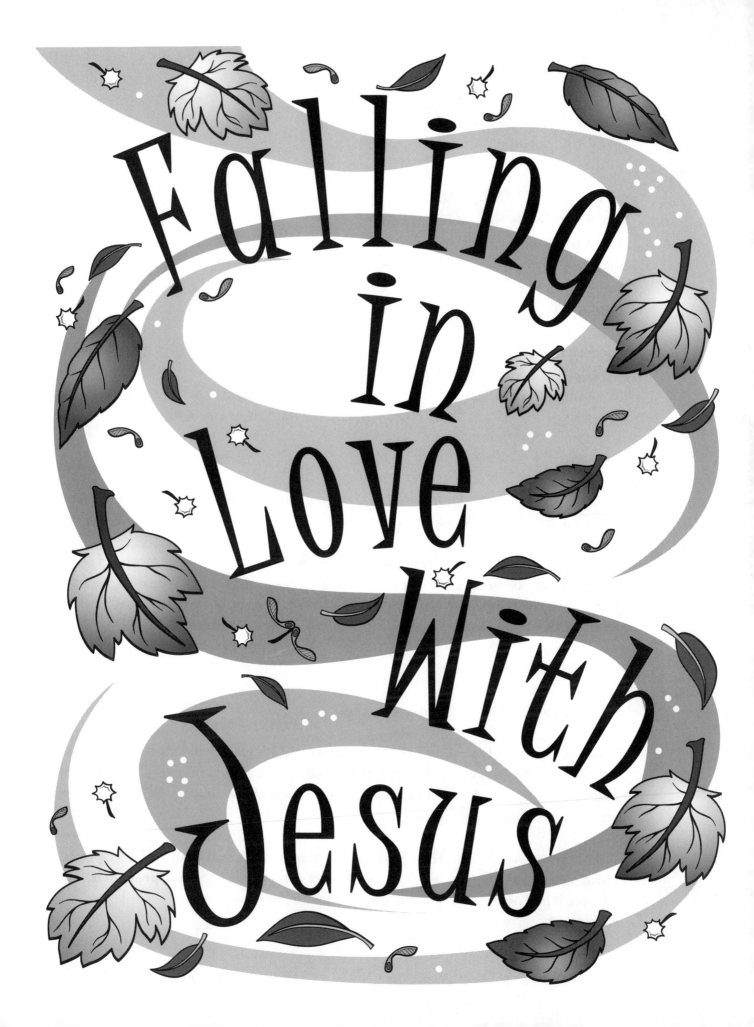

Press On

On Your Mark

Bible Truth: The Bible can help me follow God.

Bible Verse: The grass dries up. The flowers fall to the ground. But what our God says will stand forever. Isaiah 40:8

Godprint: Faith

Get Set

You'll need a pressed flower and a wilting or dead flower. Put the pressed flower inside a large Bible to mark Isaiah 40:8. You'll also need a sheet of poster board and colored markers.

GO!

Has anyone ever given you flowers? Have you ever given flowers to someone else? What kind of flowers do you like to give or receive?

We give flowers to people for special occasions like Valentine's Day or Mother's Day. When people are sick we bring a bouquet of flowers to cheer them up. Sometimes we use vases of flowers to decorate our homes or offices. Whether you pick them from your yard or garden or buy them from a flower shop, fresh flowers are beautiful!

Show children the wilting flower.

• How would you feel if someone gave you a flower that looked like this one?

This flower certainly wouldn't cheer me up much! It's wilted and shriveled and about to die. Once a flower is cut, it slowly begins to die. We can keep flowers for a few days or even a week if we put them in water. But eventually all cut flowers die. They wilt and fall over, and we throw them away.

Take out the pressed flower. **This flower is also dead, but it's still beautiful. Its color can still brighten a room. Before it wilted, when it was still fresh, someone pressed it. We could frame it and give it as a gift, and it would last a long, long time.**

Hold up the Bible.

• Which flower do you think this Bible is like? Why?

The Bible is like the pressed flower. God's Word tells us in the Book of Isaiah that "the flowers fall to the ground. But what our God says will stand forever." Every time we learn a Bible verse, we're "pressing" God's words into our hearts and minds. If we read the Bible every day, God's words won't wither or fade away from our minds. When a difficult situation comes, we'll know what to do. The Bible can help us follow God—but only if we know what it says!

Take out the poster board and quickly draw a vase with several green stems. Leave the tops of the stems empty for children to draw flowers.

Let's see how many of God's words we've pressed into our hearts. I've drawn a vase with a few empty stems. If you know a Bible verse, you may add a flower to the bouquet. Encourage children to help each other so as many children as possible can add a flower to the bouquet. It's okay if more than one child says the same verse.

What a beautiful bouquet! We'll display it in the church to encourage us all to "press on" in our study of God's Word this week.

Let's pray. Dear Lord, thank you for giving us your Word. We want to remember what your Word says. Help us to press your Word into our hearts. In Jesus' name, amen.

KSI 07/8

Knot Possible

On Your Mark

Bible Truth: Because of Jesus, nothing can separate me from God's love.

Bible Verse: Who can separate us from Christ's love? Can trouble or hard times or harm or hunger? Can nakedness or danger or war?…I am absolutely sure that not even death or life can separate us from God's love. Not even angels or demons, the present or the future, or any powers can do that. Not even the highest places or the lowest, or anything else in all creation can do that. Nothing at all can ever separate us from God's love because of what Christ Jesus our Lord has done. Romans 8:35, 38–39

Godprint: Hope

Get Set

You'll need two pieces of cotton or nylon rope or clothesline, approximately three feet long each. Tie the two pieces securely together. You'll also need a Bible.

GO!

As you tug on the two pieces of rope say, **Ugh! I'm trying to separate these two pieces of rope, but this knot is holding them together. Maybe I'm just not strong enough. Can you help me? Grab hold of the ends and pull as hard as you can.**

Invite pairs of children to take turns holding opposite ends of the knotted rope, trying to pull them apart as others cheer them on.

Wow! It doesn't seem possible to separate these two pieces of rope. It reminds me of a verse in the Bible that talks about God's love for us. Read Romans 8:35, 38–39 from a Bible. **The Bible says, "Who can separate us from Christ's love? Can trouble or hard times or harm or hunger?"**

Imagine that one piece of this rope is you and the other piece represents God's love. Jesus is like the knot that holds these two pieces of rope together. When he died on the cross for our sins and rose again from the dead, he made it possible for us to be joined to God forever.

• Let's name some hard times or troubles.

Encourage children to share. You might get them started by suggesting situations you are aware of that they may be dealing with such as sickness, difficulties at school and so on. Be prepared, however, for children who may feel free to share deep personal hurts like a parent out of work, a death in the family, or separation or divorce. Acknowledge each child's contribution as important and valid.

As each child volunteers to share a hard time or trouble, invite him or her to take one end of the rope and pull as hard as possible while you anchor the other end. When the child quits pulling, say "Nothing can separate you from God's love."

Hard times and trouble may tug and pull at us but they can never separate us from God's love. In fact, the harder we tug on the ends of these ropes, the tighter the knot gets. Life can be like that, too. Instead of separating us from God, hard times can actually make our relationship with Jesus stronger.

Let's read our Bible verses again. Read Romans 8: 35, 38–39. **Nothing can separate us from God's love. The Bible says we can be absolutely sure of it! Are you sure?** Ask the question a few times to encourage the kids to respond with a loud and enthusiastic "Yes!"

Wow! That makes me feel really good inside. It gives me hope that whatever hard times I might be facing I still have God's love. And it gives me the confidence that no matter what happens tomorrow, I can face that, too! Knowing that nothing can separate us from God's love means we don't have to worry or be afraid.

Let's pray. Dear God, thank you for never letting go of us! Thank you for being with us in every hard time we face. Thank you for a love so strong that nothing can tug us away from it. In Jesus' name we pray. Amen.

Hit or Miss?

On Your Mark

Bible Truth: God gives us the strength to do what he asks us to do.

Bible Verse: David said to Goliath, "You are coming to fight against me with a sword, a spear and a javelin. But I'm coming against you in the name of the LORD who rules over all." 1 Samuel 17:45

Godprint: Trust

Get Set

You'll need a Bible, five beanbags and masking tape. Make a one-foot square with masking tape on the floor at the front of the church. This will serve as your target. Tape a tossing line far enough from the target to make the game challenging, but still possible.

GO!

Choose three or four volunteers to toss beanbags toward the tape square on the floor. Be sure they stand behind the tossing line. Demonstrate how to toss the beanbags underhanded before kids begin.

Let's thank our volunteers with a big hand as they sit down. You all worked really hard throwing those beanbags!

• Did any of our volunteers hit the target every time?
• Did anyone hit the target the first time?

If we practiced a lot, we could get pretty good at tossing beanbags into the square. Maybe we should see if an adult with more practice could hit the target. Pull an adult "volunteer" from the congregation. Move the tossing line back far enough to make the task difficult and let the adult take a few tosses.

No matter how good we may be at something, sometimes we miss. Even the best world athletes sometimes lose a game or a meet. The Bible tells a story about someone who was a pretty good shot. He didn't use a basketball or a soccer ball or a hockey puck. He didn't even use a beanbag. He used a sling and a stone to hit an important target.

• Can you guess his name?

That's right! It's David. David was very good with his sling. He had killed a lion and a bear to protect his father's sheep. But that wasn't his most famous battle. The story we remember most is when David fought against the giant Goliath.

When David faced Goliath in battle, he didn't wear armor or carry a sword. He had no helmet on his head. He took his slingshot, picked up five smooth stones from the stream, and went off to fight Goliath. Remember, he was good at hitting a target with that slingshot.

• How important was it for David to hit the target the first time?
• What might happen to David if he missed when he shot a stone at Goliath?

David was sure he could win! Let's find out why. Ask a volunteer to read 1 Samuel 17:45.

When Goliath saw David, a young shepherd boy, coming to fight him, he thought it was going to be an easy fight. No way could this boy beat him. Not only was Goliath huge; he had armor, a helmet and some pretty powerful weapons.

• What weapons did our Bible verse say Goliath had? *(Sword, spear, javelin.)*

But David trusted in something much more powerful than swords or spears. David said that he came in the name of... *(Let the children complete the sentence: "the Lord").*

God gave David a big job to do, and David trusted God to give him the strength to do it. The same God who was with David when he faced Goliath is with us every day. When it's hard for you to follow God, remember to say, like David, "I come in the name of the Lord."

Let's stand up and say it together, so you'll be sure to remember. On the count of three, say it with me. One, two, three. All together: "I come in the name of the Lord!" Good job! This week, remember to put your trust in God and in his power, and go in the name of the Lord.

Let's pray. Dear powerful God, thank you for the jobs you give us to do, and thank you for the strength you give us to do them. Help us to trust in your power. In Jesus' name, amen.

Out of My Way, I'm Coming Through

On Your Mark

Bible Truth: God wants us to trust Jesus and not to let anything get in the way of following him.

Bible Verse: A huge cloud of witnesses is all around us. So let us throw off everything that stands in our way. Let us throw off any sin that holds on to us so tightly. Let us keep on running the race marked out for us. Let us keep looking to Jesus. Hebrews 12:1–2

Godprint: Integrity

Get Set

You'll need a Bible, a stopwatch for timing and items for a short obstacle course. Set up the course at the front of the church using several easily moveable items, such as chairs or boxes, that the children can safely climb over, walk around or crawl under. Mark the start and finish lines with masking tape on the floor.

GO!

Did you notice something different up here at the front today? What do you think this is? An obstacle course!

• Who can tell us what an obstacle is? (*Something that gets in your way, something hard to get around.*)

An obstacle is something that keeps you from getting where you want to be. So an obstacle course is like a race track with things that you have to go around, go over or go through.

Select three volunteers to run the course. Quickly explain the course to your volunteers, showing them what to go over, under and around.

You're going to be working as a team to see how much time it takes for all three of you to get through the course. There are a couple of rules to remember. First, no running or jumping—just fast walking or crawling. Second, you may not start until the person ahead of you has crossed the finish line.

Turn to the rest of the children. **You have an important job, too. Racers always do better when people are cheering them on. So, while our racers are going through the course, you can encourage them by clapping and cheering.**

Time the three volunteers, starting the timer when the first begins and stopping when the third finishes.

Wow! That was pretty fast. You did that in _____ (give the time from the stopwatch). **Let's give them a big hand. Now, what if we took away the obstacles? Could you get from start to finish faster? Let's try it.** Quickly remove the obstacles and time the children again. Remind them of the two rules before they start.

Thank you so much! Let's give them a big hand while they sit down.

• Do you think the second time was faster? (Give the actual time.) Why was it faster?

The Bible has something to say about running a race. Let's look at one of the verses that talks about a crowd cheering on the runners.

Open your Bible and read Hebrews 12:1 and the first phrase of verse 2.

• How do you feel when people watch you in a race or a sports game?
• Can you hear your mom and dad cheering for you when you play soccer or another game?
• What kinds of things keep you from doing your best in a race?
• While some of you ran our obstacle course, what did the rest of you do? (Cheered them on.)

This verse says that we have a huge cloud of witnesses while we run our race for Jesus. These people have run the race for Jesus, too, and they know how hard it can be. They want us to be able to focus on Jesus and keep running. Some of these people are in heaven, like Abraham and Moses and Paul. But some of them are right here, like your friends around you and all of the grown-ups here at church.

I want all of our grown-ups to stand up. Pause to encourage the congregation to stand. **If you promise to help show these kids how to run the race for Jesus, give me a loud "Amen!"** Pause for response. **If you promise to encourage these kids as they run their race for Jesus, give me a loud "Amen!"**

Turn back to the kids. **When things get tough, remember that there are people here at church who will help you run your race for Jesus.**

Let's pray. Dear Jesus, thank you for showing us how to run the race. Thank you for the people who give us examples of how to run the race of faith. Help us to be faithful to you. In your name we pray, amen.

True Colors

On Your Mark

Bible Truth: God wants us to honor him in our thoughts.

Bible Verse: Think about things that are in heaven. Don't think about things that are on earth. Colossians 3:2

Godprint: Loyalty

Get Set

You'll need a colored fall leaf for each child. If colored leaves aren't available in your area, cut different-colored leaf shapes out of construction paper. Put the fall leaves in a basket. You'll also need a few green leaves or leaf shapes and a Bible.

GO!

I can tell fall is coming. The air is getting colder, the days are getting shorter and the leaves are falling from the trees.

Dump the basket of fall leaves onto the children. Help each child find a leaf.

Look at these beautiful fall leaves! What colors are on each leaf? How many different colors do we have?

Fall is one of the most colorful times of year—because of leaves. In the fall, leaves turn from their usual green to every shade of red, yellow, orange, brown and even purple. Each tree has its own unique leaf shape and its own range of colors. Aspen leaves are small and round. They usually turn bright golden yellow. Maple leaves have pointy "fingers." They turn all shades of orange and red. Plum leaves are long and narrow. They turn red and purple.

• Can anyone guess what kind of tree your leaf came from?

Leaves are amazing. Did you know leaves make food for their trees? Trees take in water through their roots and carbon dioxide from the air. Leaves use the sunlight to turn the carbon dioxide and water into a kind of sugar called glucose. That's what trees and other plants eat. They need it to grow, and without leaves they couldn't get it. The whole process is called photosynthesis. You may have learned about it in school. But let me

tell you something else about leaves. Hold up the green leaves.

• What color are these leaves?
• What makes the leaves green? (Older children may know about chlorophyll.)

These leaves are green because they have chlorophyll. Chlorophyll is the chemical that helps leaves do their jobs, and chlorophyll is green.

• What happens to leaves in the fall?
• Why do they change colors?

In the fall and winter, when the days are shorter and the weather is colder, there isn't enough light for leaves to make food. So in the fall leaves rest. They stop making food and let their trees live off of the glucose that was stored in the spring and summer. The green chlorophyll disappears, and the leaves turn beautiful colors like the leaves you're holding now.

• What's the true color of a leaf?

The beautiful leaves we see in the fall are showing their true colors. The yellows, oranges and reds were there all along. They're just covered by chlorophyll sometimes. Hold up the green leaves again. **These green leaves look a lot alike. But the leaves you're holding are all different. In the fall, when they show their true colors, no two leaves are exactly alike.**

As you go back to school this fall, you may be tempted to "blend in" and try to be like everyone else. You might want to think about the same things that are important to everyone else. But God wants you to show your "true colors." If you belong to him, he wants you to think about things that are really important, not just what everyone else thinks about.

Listen to what the Bible says. Read Colossians 3:2 from a Bible or ask a confident reader to do it.

• What are some things that are in heaven for us to think about?
• How can you think about things that are in heaven while you're at school?

Instead of trying to blend in this fall, show your true colors. That's what makes fall beautiful, and that's how we can be beautiful, too.

Let's pray. Dear God, you made every leaf that we're holding in our hands right now, and you made each one of us. Help us to show our true colors by thinking about the things you want us to think about. In Jesus' name, amen.

Generations

On Your Mark

Bible Truth: God gives us people to help us learn about him.

Bible Verse: God, ever since I was young you have taught me about what you have done. To this very day I tell about your wonderful acts. God, don't leave me even when I'm old and have gray hair. Let me live to tell my children about your power. Let me tell all of them about your mighty acts. Psalm 71:17–18

Godprint: Community

Get Set

You'll need several family photos, including young children, parents and grandparents. If possible, include a photo of yourself as a child. You'll also need scissors, construction paper, markers and a stapler. Cut the construction paper into 1x6-inch strips.

GO!

Show the family pictures, beginning with the childhood photo. Modify the text below as needed to incorporate personal details about your growth to adulthood, such as marriage, glasses, gray hair and so on.

Can you guess who this kid is? Yep, I was once a little kid like all of you. But I didn't stay little, did I? I grew older and taller. As I grew, I learned. I learned things at school from my teachers.

• What are some things you've learned at school this week?

At home, I learned things from my parents and grandparents.

• What are some things your parents, grandparents or other family members have taught you?

Parents and grandparents are special people, aren't they? Grandparents Day is a special day when we honor our grandparents. But the special relationships we have with grandparents last all year long. Grandparents love us very much, and they can teach us all sorts of things. They teach us skills when they share hobbies like knitting or fishing or baking bread. They teach us history when they tell us what life was like when they were younger.

Parents and grandparents can also teach us about God. They can read or tell us Bible stories and take us to church. When we have parents or grandparents who follow God, we can learn by imitating their godly actions.

• What things do your parents or grandparents do that show they're following God?

In the Book of Psalms, the psalmist asks God to help him tell his children and grandchildren about God's goodness and power. Invite a volunteer to read Psalm 71:17–18 from a Bible.

Whether we're young or old, we're all part of a family. And everyone here in this room is part of God's family, the church. So let's spend a few minutes of "family time" celebrating the good things that God has done.

I'm going to give each one of you two paper strips and a marker. Depending on the number of children, the size of your congregation and the time you have, you can adjust the number of strips you hand out. I want you to find two people who are parents or grandparents. Ask them to write on a paper strip something wonderful that God has done. This could be something personal that's happened in their families, something God has done for our church family, or something that happened in Bible times. When you're finished, bring the strips back to me. Is everyone ready? Tell all about God's wonderful acts!

Allow a few minutes for kids to find people to write. As they bring the completed strips back to you, invite kids to help you staple the strips into one long paper chain. Have the children hold up the chain in a center aisle or another visible location.

Look how long our chain is! From generation to generation—children, parents and grandparents—we're all connected by God's goodness. This week, watch for the "wonderful acts" God will do. When you notice what God has done, don't forget to tell someone!

Let's pray. Dear God, you are wonderful and you do wonderful things. Help us remember to tell about your wonderful acts so that no one will ever forget them. Amen.

Tiny Treasures

On Your Mark

Bible Truth: God is everywhere. We can find him everywhere we look.

Bible Verse: The kingdom of heaven is like treasure that was hidden in a field. When a man found it, he hid it again. He was very happy. So he went and sold everything he had. And he bought that field. Matthew 13:44

Godprint: Joy

Get Set

You'll need several large red apples in a brown bag, a paring knife and a Bible. Optional: a cutting board you can hold in your lap.

GO!

If you wanted to find a treasure, where would you look? Have several children make guesses. Pull out the brown bag.

• Does this look like the kind of place where we could find a treasure?

I am going to pass this bag around the group. See if you can guess what is inside without looking. Remember, we're looking for a treasure. But it's probably not something you would expect. No peeking! Fold the top of the bag closed and pass the bag around the circle. Let each child make a guess. Some of the children will figure out that the bag holds apples, or some kind of fruit.

Let's find out if we guessed right. Invite a child to reach into the bag and pull out an apple.

• What kind of treasure is an apple?
• What kind of treasure might be inside this apple?

Use the paring knife to cut the apple in half crosswise so you expose the star made of seeds. Hold the apple star up for children to see. Pass the apple around for the children to hold and investigate.

We found a hidden treasure! Jesus talked about a hidden treasure. Let's read a verse about a hidden treasure.

Read Matthew 13:44 from a Bible or ask a confident reader to do so.

• What did the man find in the field? *(A hidden treasure.)*
• What did the man do? *(Sold everything to buy the field so he could keep the treasure.)*
• What did Jesus say the treasure was like? *(The kingdom of heaven.)*

The man knew that the treasure was so valuable that he would do everything he could to have it. So he sold everything he owned and bought the field where he found the treasure. The kingdom of heaven is like that. God wants us to find the treasure of his kingdom, just like we found the treasure inside this apple. And once we find the treasure, we want to keep it.

Hold up the apple star again. **God put a little reminder of himself in the middle of this apple. When we see this star, we can remember that God made the apple and God made everything in the world. God made each of us and wants us to be part of his kingdom.**

Cut the additional apples into wedges and pass them out to the children. **The next time you eat an apple, I hope you'll think of the treasure we found hidden inside the apple today. Then remember that the kingdom of heaven, God's kingdom, is the most valuable treasure we could ever find.**

Let's pray. Thank you, God, for all the treasures, big and little, that you have given us. Thank you for your kingdom and inviting us to be part of it. In Jesus' name, amen.

What's That Smell?

On Your Mark

Bible Truth: God wants us to show Jesus in our lives.

Bible Verse: Through us, God spreads the knowledge of Christ everywhere like perfume. God considers us to be the sweet smell that Christ is spreading among people who are being saved and people who are dying. 2 Corinthians 2:14–15

Godprint: Evangelism

Get Set

You'll need a Bible, a scented candle, candleholder and matches.

GO!

Guess what I have here? Show the candle. **Who wants to guess what it smells like?** Listen to answers. **Now, if your mom had a candle like this at your house and she wanted everyone to smell that nice smell when they came in the door, would she run up to them and have them take a sniff?**

Put the candle under several children's noses saying, **Here, smell my nice candle. Here, smell my nice candle. No, she wouldn't do that! What would she do if she wanted the house to smell nice, like the candle? She would light it!** Light the candle and set it somewhere safe to burn. **We'll let our candle sit there a minute and see if we can smell its nice scent.**

- What do you smell now?
- Did we smell the candle more before we lit it or after? *(After.)*

The candle smells the strongest when it is losing some of itself. See? The wick is burning shorter and there is less wax now than before we lit the candle.

Did you know that the Bible says God wants us to be like this candle? It's true! God says he wants us to smell good to people. Read 2 Corinthians 2:14, starting with the last phrase of the verse and continue through verse 15.

- What does God say we smell like? *(We smell like perfume.)*

• Who's supposed to smell our perfume? *(The people around us.)*
• What would happen if we stayed far away from the candle? Would we ever be able to smell it? *(No, we need to be near it.)*

If people are going to find out about Jesus, they have to be near people who know Jesus.

• What kinds of things can you do to be around people who need to know Jesus? *(Invite a friend home from school to play. Ask neighbors over for dinner. Be friendly to people in the grocery store, the doctor's office, everywhere!)*

Sometimes we can smell good for Jesus if we give up something, just like the candle gives up part of itself. Smelling good to people isn't always easy, but that good smell in our lives can help others see Jesus. Talk about Jesus, be around people and help people the way Jesus did. Pretty soon people will be asking, "What's that smell?" You'll smell different. Your life will "smell" like who? Like Jesus!

Let's pray. Dear Jesus, we want to smell good for you! Help us to be willing to give up a part of ourselves so that other people can know you better. In your name, amen.

The Wheels on the Bus Go 'Round and 'Round

On Your Mark

Bible Truth: God wants us to welcome other people.

Bible Verse: So we should welcome people like them. We should work together with them for the truth. 3 John 8

Godprint: Kindness

Get Set

You'll need a Bible and two or three wool mufflers or scarves.

GO!

Machines. They make a lot of noise, don't they? Give me your best lawn mower imitation, please. Allow kids to do their thing!

Super job. Now how about the engine of a school bus? Pause for kids to respond. **Hmm. That one sounds like it needs a little tuning. Maybe it needs a brand new muffler.** Take the wool mufflers you brought with you and fold them gently around the children closest to you! **Now try it again.** Pause and listen. **Oh, much, much better!**

Machines have lots of parts that must work together for the whole thing to run well. Let's think of all the parts that a "welcome wagon" might need to do its job of welcoming others. Let's start with the engine.

• Why is an engine important?

Without the engine our welcome wagon wouldn't do much of anything. Point to the children on your right. The children on the left and in the middle will get their turns later. **This group here will be the gears and gizmos of our "welcome wagon" engine. Let's hear what it sounds like.**

Good! Remember to "start your engine" this fall and welcome someone new to school. Give a smile! Say hello. Share your cupcake. Remember that when you welcome others, you welcome Jesus!

• How about wheels? Why does our "welcome wagon" need wheels?

Once the engine starts and the gizmos inside crank up, the wheels help the wagon get moving.

Point to the group of kids to your left. **Give me the sound of our "welcome wagon" wheels in action.** Pause. **Super! You can help others feel welcome by "turning your wheels" and thinking of ways to make them feel at home in school.**

• Who can tell me one way to make other kids feel comfortable at school? *(Share a lunch, buddy up and walk to school, play soccer.)*

What else do we need on our "welcome wagon?" Oh, yes! The horn! Point to the children in the middle. **How might a horn sound on our "welcome wagon?"** Pause. **Stupendous! Remember to toot your horn to welcome newcomers. Say, "Welcome to school!" or "I'm glad you're here!" Jesus didn't have fancy equipment to help him spread his heavenly message. Be like him and let your tongue do the talking!**

Now let's get our "welcome wagon" moving noisily along. This is the brake. Hold your fists in the air. **When I pull it** *(pull your fists to your chest)* **our wagon must come to a screeching halt. Ready to make your "welcome wagon" sounds? Go!** Enjoy the cacophony of sounds. Then pull the brake. **I think you've got it!**

God wants us to work together to welcome others and to spread his Word. Wherever Jesus went, into towns and villages, he taught and preached the good news. He did everything he could to make people feel welcome in his Father's kingdom. Like well-oiled machines, we can work together to help others the way Jesus did.

Let's pray. Help us, Jesus, to welcome each other and to work together. As we start a new year of school, help us welcome new friends. Amen.

Better Together

On Your Mark

Bible Truth: God wants us to work together to serve him.

Bible Verse: There is one body. But it has many parts. Even though it has many parts, they make up one body. It is the same with Christ. 1 Corinthians 12:12

Godprint: Community

Get Set

You'll need a Bible, a cookie or brownie for each child, a container for the cookies or brownies, and zip-top snack bags, each containing a single ingredient found in the cookie or brownie recipe: flour, salt, baking powder, baking soda, vanilla, butter, white sugar, brown sugar, baking cocoa and a broken egg.

GO!

Be careful not to let the children see the cookies or brownies until the end!

I have a bunch of goodies with me today. Look at these little bags. Who can guess what might be in this bag? Hold up each one individually and let the children guess the contents. Tell them what the bags hold if they can't guess.

• What do you think these things are used for? (Cooking.)
• Why do I have this group of foods with me and not different ones? (They make something when you mix them together.)
• Who wants to guess what it is you can make from these foods? (Take guesses until someone is right or comes close.)

Right! These are the ingredients for homemade cookies (or brownies). **Do any of you like cookies? Me, too. Let's taste our ingredients to see if our cookies will be good. Would you help me?** Ask children you know will be cooperative to dip a licked finger into a bag that you are holding open and lick off the ingredient stuck on it. Do not use the raw egg, but instead say, **This egg isn't good to eat raw, is it? We won't try this one because we already know it isn't good.** Put each bag aside after one child taste tests it.

• How did the vanilla taste?   • How about the baking soda?

- The baking cocoa?
- The flour?
- The baking powder?

- The butter?
- The sugars?
- The salt?

Did they mostly taste good, or bad? *Bad!* **But how can that be? We like cookies.**

The foods in the bags aren't cookies, are they? They are the ingredients to make cookies. Before we get cookies we need to mix all these things together and cook them.

- What would happen if we tried to make cookies but left out the eggs or the flour? *(They wouldn't come out right; they would taste bad; they would fall apart.)*

- What if we left out a small ingredient, one that you use very little of in the recipe, like salt or vanilla? *(They wouldn't taste the best; they'd miss some flavor.)*

Right. We could bake the cookies that way, but without all the ingredients, they wouldn't be as good. The Bible tells us that God gives each one of us special talents and abilities. God calls those things his gifts to us. There are special ways that God makes each of us and special ways he wants each of us to serve him. Those gifts are like our ingredients. You might be flour, I might be butter, you might be salt or sugar.

- Do our ingredients taste best left alone or combined together? *(Together.)*

Listen to what God says in 1 Corinthians 12:12. Read the verse from a Bible. **Now, let's put our cooking words in this verse. There is one cookie. But it has many ingredients. Even though it has many ingredients, they make up one cookie. It is the same with Christ.**

God wants us to join together with people who love him to help and serve others. We could do it alone, but which tastes better, the ingredients by themselves *(show bags)* **or the ingredients all mixed together to form cookies? Whatever gift you have from God, it's better when you mix it with other people's gifts.**

Let's pray and ask God to help us work together to serve him. Dear God, we love you and want to be ingredients for your work. Mix us together in just the right way to serve you best. In Jesus' name, amen.

Would you like to eat these ingredients *(show bags)* **or one of these real cookies?** Pass out treats to the kids.

Feasting at His Table

On Your Mark

Bible Truth: God deserves our thanks and praise.

Bible Verse: Give thanks to the LORD, because he is good. His faithful love continues forever. Psalm 136:1

Godprint: Thankfulness

Get Set

You'll need a Bible and a large basket or box. A week or two ahead of time, ask families to bring canned food to share. Optional: Gather a basket of canned goods on your own or use some items from your church's food pantry.

GO!

Thanksgiving Day is coming, and I can't wait. I just love Thanksgiving dinner. There's turkey, mashed potatoes, stuffing, cranberry sauce and lots of yummy vegetables. But do you know what my favorite Thanksgiving food is? Pie. Describe your favorite Thanksgiving pie or other dessert. **What's your favorite part of Thanksgiving dinner? Raise your hands if I name something you really like.**

• Who likes turkey?
• Who likes cranberry sauce?
• Who likes potatoes?
• Who likes dessert?

I think Thanksgiving is the greatest feast of the whole year! But Thanksgiving isn't just about food, is it? Thanksgiving is really about being thankful.

• What are some things you're thankful for?

Great! We know what foods we like, and we know what we're thankful for. Now I have a trickier question.

• Why do we celebrate a day for giving thanks with a big feast?

In Old Testament times, God's people celebrated with feasts to remember the good things that God had done. There was the Feast of Trumpets on the first day of the seventh month. It was a holiday—like Thanksgiving—when people rested from their work. They also had a special worship service that was announced with trumpet blasts. Can I hear some trumpet blasts right now? Pause and let kids blast imaginary trumpets.

The Passover feast reminded the people how God delivered them from slavery in Egypt. People still celebrate Passover today. It's a special meal that's the same every year—just like Thanksgiving.

But I think the feast that's most like Thanksgiving was the Feast of Booths. Listen to what the Bible says about the Feast of Booths. Invite a volunteer to read Deuteronomy 16:13–15.

• How long did this feast last? *(Seven days.)*

Can you imagine how full you'd be if our Thanksgiving feast lasted for seven days? My tummy hurts just thinking about it! The Israelites' tummies must have been full of food. But their hearts were full of joy as they celebrated God's goodness.

Feasts like Thanksgiving are special times for families to celebrate their joys and thank God for his blessings. Feasts are also times to share joy with others who may not have as much as we do. Right now I'd like you to take a minute or two to gather with your families. Thank God for the good things he's done for your family, then share your joy by sharing a can of food with the hungry people in our community.

Allow a few minutes for families to share, then collect the cans. Or, let children explore the basket of food items you gathered ahead of time and talk about how these items will share joy with the families who receive them.

Let's thank God by reading Psalm 136 together. You can be the leaders for the congregation's part. Read Psalm 136 responsively with the congregation speaking the second part of each verse: "His faithful love continues forever." If time allows, encourage families to add their own thanksgivings to the psalmist's.

God deserves our thanks and praise this Thanksgiving and on every day throughout the year. Enjoy the feast!

Donate the canned food to a local food bank.

Constellations

On Your Mark

Bible Truth: God is in charge of everything.

Bible Verse: Look up toward the sky. Who created everything you see? The LORD causes the stars to come out at night one by one. He gives each one of them a name. His power and strength are great. So none of the stars is missing. Isaiah 40:26

Godprint: Wonder

Get Set

You'll need a Bible, an illustration of the Big Dipper *(see page 32)*, black poster board and sticks of white chalk. Optional: star stickers.

GO!

Have you ever looked up at the sky on a summer night? What do you see? Pause to listen to answers.

On a clear night, the sky seems to be filled with stars. Sometimes stars shine so brightly we feel like we could reach out and touch them. They can seem so close, but they're actually far, far away. Because they're so far away, the stars we see in the sky look like tiny white dots. But stars are actually really, really big. And they can be many different colors—blue, yellow, red and orange.

• What do we call a group of stars that seem to make a picture? (*A constellation.*)

Show the Big Dipper illustration.

• Does anyone recognize what this is? (*Congratulate any children who recognized the Big Dipper.*)

We call this group of stars, or constellation, the Big Dipper. How do you think this group of stars got that name? Pause to let the kids speculate.

The Big Dipper reminds people of a big soup spoon. It has a bent "handle" with three stars and a "bowl" with four stars. Other "constellations" or groups of stars have shapes like animals or people.

Let's see if we can make our own "constellation" on this black "night sky."

Give children pieces of white chalk and/or star stickers. Have each child place a star sticker or draw a dot on the black poster board. When children have all made their stars, use a piece of chalk to connect them. If you have time, you can invite children to make the connections.

• If you could name your star, what would you name it?
• What does our constellation remind you of?

People have always been interested in the stars. They even named the stars in the Big Dipper. The two stars at the end of the Big Dipper's bowl are named Merak and Dubhe. They're known as pointer stars because they point to the North Star, Polaris. Sailors still use the North Star to help them find their way across the sea. If they're sailing toward Polaris, they're sailing north. If they're sailing away from Polaris, they're sailing south.

I think all the stars in the sky are pointer stars. They point us to God. God created all the stars. And the Bible says he has a name for each one—even the ones that are too far away for us to see or even know about. Read Isaiah 40:26 from a Bible or ask a confident reader to do it.

Not one star is missing. Our whole universe is set up just the way God wants it. From the massive stars in the sky to the tiny hairs on our heads, God is in charge of everything. Let's thank him now for being such an amazing God.

Let's pray. God, you made every wonderful star in the night sky. When we think of the stars, we think of you. Thank you for giving us the stars to point to you. In Jesus' name, amen.

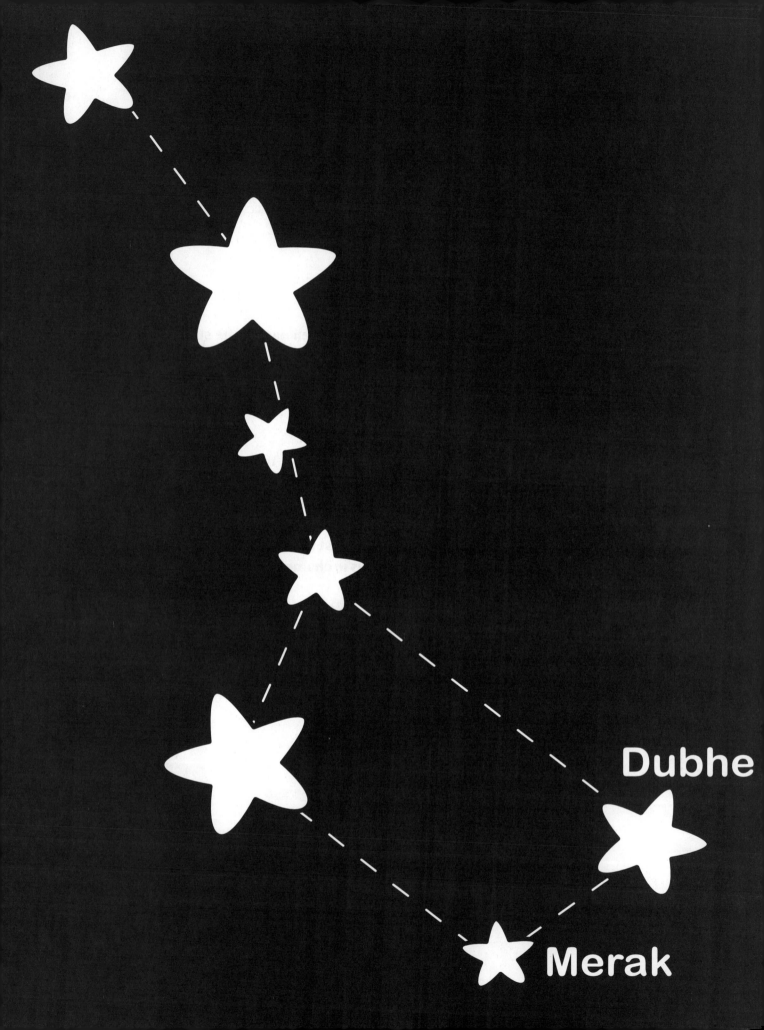

Shivers, Chills and Frost

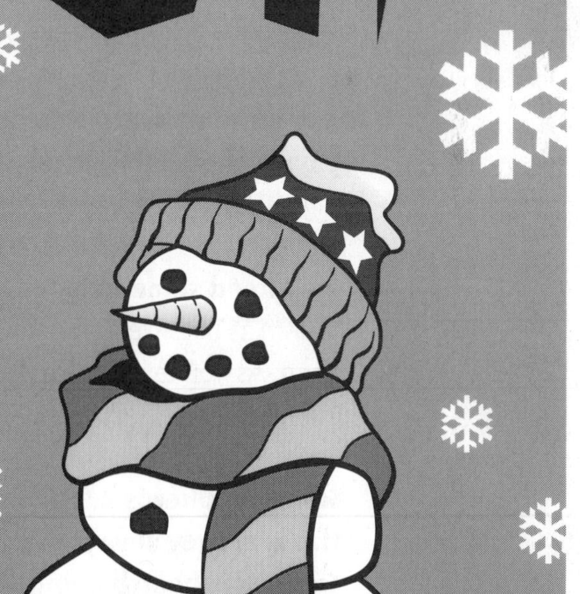

Jesus: The Fabric of Our Lives

On Your Mark

Bible Truth: God sent his Son to be the Savior of the world.

Bible Verse: But the angel said to them, "Do not be afraid. I bring you good news of great joy. It is for all the people. Today in the town of David a Savior has been born to you. He is Christ the Lord. Here is how you will know I am telling you the truth. You will find a baby wrapped in strips of cloth and lying in a manger. Luke 2:10–12.

Godprint: Joy

Get Set

You'll need a brightly colored piece of fabric, about 1' x 3', and a Bible.

GO!

Keep the fabric out of sight as you begin. **You've all heard the story of the birth of Jesus many times. Maybe you've even read it in the Bible for yourselves.**

• What's your favorite part of the Christmas story? *(Angels, shepherds, wise men, manger and so on.)*

Today we're going to talk about one part of the Christmas story. I have something behind my back that will help us. Can you guess what it is? Let the children make a few guesses, then bring out the fabric.

I may need some help with the fabric today. Will you be ready if I need you? Use as many children as possible in the story. Look for the child who would like to participate but may be too shy to say so. As you tell each segment of the story, use the fabric as a prop. If you prefer, let the children prompt the next part of the story and adapt how you use the fabric to fit their suggestions.

Some shepherds were out in the field at night. They were taking care of their sheep, just the way they always did. Place the fabric on the head of a child to represent a shepherd. **Let me hear the sheep baa-ing. Baa!**

This night was an ordinary night—at least that's what the shepherds thought. Perhaps they had a fire and took turns staying awake. Suddenly an angel appeared, right there in the

night. Wave the fabric through the air dramatically and make it land on the shoulders of another child.
• Who can tell us what the angel said to the shepherds. *("Don't be afraid.")*
• What do you think the shepherds thought?

Let's find out exactly what else the angel said. Read Luke 2:10–12 from a Bible. **Wow! The angel had some amazing news!**

• How would the shepherds know that what the angel said was true? *(They would find the baby lying in a manger, just as they said.)*

The shepherds hurried off to Bethlehem—the town of David that the angel talked about. They found the place where Jesus was born. Mary and Joseph were there. They had traveled from the town they lived in. God wanted Jesus to be born in Bethlehem, and he had chosen Mary to bring the most wonderful gift for all of us into the world. Place the fabric on one child's head to represent Mary.

And there, in the manger, just as the angel said, the shepherds found the baby Jesus. Wrap the fabric around the arm of one child and cradle it like a baby.

The shepherds were just ordinary people, living ordinary lives. Suddenly they found themselves right in the middle of a miracle.

We may feel like we are ordinary people, leading ordinary lives too. But we can be part of the miracle of Jesus as well. We don't have to journey to Bethlehem to find him. Wrap the Bible in the fabric. **We only need to look right here. God's Word tells us all about the angels, and the shepherds, and Mary and Joseph, and the baby Jesus. Most of all, God's Word tells us how much God loves us and why he sent his Son to be born in a manger and be the Savior of the world.**

After the shepherds saw the baby, they went out and told everyone they knew what had happened. I hope that as Christmas gets closer and closer, you'll find someone to share the good news of Jesus with.

Let's pray. Dear God, thank you for sending your Son. Thank you for sending the angel to tell the shepherds the good news. Thank you for helping the shepherds tell the good news to everyone they knew. Help us to share the good news too. In Jesus' name, amen.

Gingerbread Smiles

On Your Mark

Bible Truth: God wants us to work together to spread the message of Jesus.

Bible Verse: They have spent all their time serving God's people. Brothers and sisters, I am asking you to follow the lead of people like them. Follow everyone who joins in the task and works hard at it. 1 Corinthians 16:15–16

Godprint: Community

Get Set

You'll need a brown grocery sack, scissors, a Bible, thin-tipped marker, mini-gingerbread man cookies. Optional: Gingerbread man cookie cutter, glitter glue.

GO!

Hold up the paper sack. **How can one of these come in handy especially this time of year?** Listen to responses.

I didn't realize all that could be done with one paper bag! Let's see. We use paper bags to bring home the Christmas treasures we make at school. Bags can hold the special holiday fixings for our Christmas feast—maybe even a box or two of delicious gingerbread cookies!

Hold up the package of gingerbread men cookies. **And at the department store, the clerk can easily fill our bag with holiday lights, candles and decorations. This bag is such a help. I'm glad I have it.**

Do you know what else is a big, big help this time of year? You are! We can help each other!

• How do you help your family at Christmas?

As kids offer responses, pick up the scissors and cut out one long rectangular side strip from the paper sack (16 1/2" x 7").

• Does the job of getting ready for Christmas go faster if everyone lends a hand? Why?
• How does helping your family make you feel good inside?

Accordion-fold the long paper strip four times, paper doll style. Crease the edge.

Yes! Yes! Yes! There are so many ways we can help others! Pick out a tree. Help hang all the sparkling balls. Mix a delicious Christmas punch or bake a batch of cookies. Jesus is so happy when we join together to celebrate his birthday. It means we have given him in a special place in our hearts.

Mary and Joseph must have been so happy to have a beautiful, bouncy baby boy. Do we have any beautiful, bouncy babies in our congregation today? Ask moms or dads to stand and show off their beautiful babies. **Baby Jesus probably looked a lot like one of these! Thank you, moms and dads.**

Draw a gingerbread man on the top layer of the folded paper. If you use a cookie cutter, trace the outline. Make sure the hands and feet extend to the folded edges.

Ask an older child to read 1 Corinthians 16:15–16.

Jesus wants us to join him and each other to help spread his message of peace, love and hope to the world. What joy we feel when we're part of a family that works together in love!

Hold the accordion folds in one hand and cut out the gingerbread man outline with the other. Do not cut where the hands and feet touch the folded edge.

The Christmas message is one that every person on earth needs to hear. If we all work together, we can get the message out!

Open the paper to reveal five gingerbread children all joined together. If you wish, use the glitter glue to dot eyes, noses and great big holiday smiles.

Let's pray. Thank you, God, for giving us the baby Jesus. Help us join together to serve him and help others.

Pass out the mini-gingerbread man cookies. If you have enough cookies, give each child two, one to eat and one to share with a pew buddy.

Time for a Heart Check

winter

On Your Mark

Bible Truth: God wants us to know and please Jesus.

Bible Verse: But make sure in your hearts that Christ is Lord. 1 Peter 3:15

Godprint: Faith

Get Set

You'll need a Bible, a paper grocery bag with a large red heart colored on the blank side and various children's toys and objects to fill the bag to the top. Customize this list to match the children in your church. Possibilities include: soccer ball, toys, video games, movies, CDs, school books, coloring books and so on. If you'd like, you could include one or two items to represent adults, such as a day planner or a set of keys.

GO!

We have a great Bible verse to talk about today. It comes from 1 Peter 3:15. Let's hear what God says to us. Read the first line of the verse from a Bible: "But make sure in your hearts that Christ is Lord."

• Who is this verse talking about? *(God, Jesus.)*
• Who is Christ? *(Jesus.)*

Sometimes the Bible says "Jesus," sometimes "Christ" and sometimes "Jesus Christ." Jesus is a first name, like Joshua or Nathan. Christ is a title, like the principal or the doctor. In this case it means the Savior. If there were other people named Jesus, and you said "Christ," people would know you were talking about Jesus the Savior. So when we see the word "Christ" in the Bible, we know it's talking about Jesus.

• What does this verse say to do with Jesus? (Make sure he is Lord.)

"Lord" means the one who rules over everything. If we lived in a country with a king, the king would be lord of the land. He would control everything in his kingdom. Well, the Bible tells us that's Jesus' place. He should be the ruler of our hearts. He should have first place in our lives.

I brought along a sample of our hearts today and I thought you kids could help me give our heart a check-up. Here's our heart. Show the bag, heart side facing the children. **Let's take a look inside. Remember, we're looking inside to see if Jesus is ruling our hearts; to see whether he is number one in our lives.**

Begin pulling out one object at a time and making a brief comment like: **A truck. Who here likes trucks? Playing with trucks is fun, but where's Jesus? A soccer ball. I'm sure a lot of you play soccer. It's a fast sport and good exercise, but where's Jesus?** Finish your comment about each object with "but where's Jesus?" If you are using items to represent adult busyness, ask kids to name grown-ups they know who use those things, then tell you about why those items are so important to the grown-ups. You could say, **Even grown-ups have a hard time making room for Jesus.** The congregation listening in will get your point!

Show the empty bag. **Look, our heart is empty now and there was no Jesus. Being with our families and friends and playing games and taking trips are wonderful things to do. Jesus wants us to be happy and to have fun. But sometimes we are so busy with all the other things that we aren't saving a place for him. There's no time left in our day and no room left in our hearts.**

First Peter 3:15 says *make sure* **there's room for Jesus. When Jesus was born, there was no room for him at the inn. But that little baby was the Lord of everything. Don't let your life get so filled up that there is no time for him.**

• If Jesus is first in our lives, which of these things should we put first inside our hearts? *(The Bible.)*

Place the Bible inside the empty bag. **Remember, make sure Jesus is first!**

Let's pray. Dear Jesus, we want you to be first in our hearts! Help us to always make sure you have first place. Be the Lord of our lives. In your name we pray, amen.

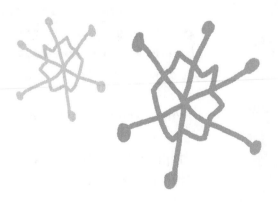

Hibernation

On Your Mark

Bible Truth: We don't always understand how God works, but we can always trust him.

Bible Verse: It is written, "No eye has seen, no ear has heard, no mind has known what God has prepared for those who love him." 1 Corinthians 2:9

Godprint: Trust

Get Set

You'll need a Bible and a bag of unshelled peanuts. Before the service, hide the nuts around the front of the church. Set the bag aside to collect the nuts later.

GO!

Winter is coming!

• What are some signs that let us know winter is on its way? *(It gets cold. People wear heavy coats and hats and mittens. Sometimes it snows.)*

Animals get ready for winter, too. Furry animals get thicker fur. Some birds get an extra layer of downy feathers. Chipmunks, bears and other animals gather food and store it to eat later. I've hidden some winter chipmunk food at the front of the church. Let's see if we can find it and gather it up.

Encourage children to gather the nuts and put them in the bag.

Good job, chipmunks. You're almost ready for winter. You'll also want to eat some of this extra food so you can get nice and fat. Let's toss some food out to the bears and chipmunks in the congregation. Gently toss a couple of handful of nuts to adults listening in. If you'd like, let kids open the nuts and munch while you continue.

• Why do you suppose chipmunks would want to get fatter in the winter? *(Listen to responses.)*

Chipmunks store the extra food they eat as body fat. They use the fat for energy while they hibernate.

• What do you know about hibernation? *(Listen to responses.)*

Chipmunks and some other animals *hibernate* for part or all of the winter. Hibernation is a special, very deep sleep. The chipmunk's body temperature drops, and its heartbeat and breathing slow down. It uses very little energy. Let's pretend we're hibernating now. Everyone lie down and breathe very slowly.

Let children lie down and pretend to hibernate for a few moments. Include a few snores just for fun.

Okay chipmunks, time to wake up. Spring has sprung and your little bodies are ready to go again!

Hibernation is one of God's amazing plans for his animal creations. The animals don't eat for three whole months, but they don't starve to death. They know just how many nuts to eat to store up the extra fat they'll need. Their bodies get colder, but not so cold that they freeze. Somehow they know just when winter is over and it's time to wake up.

God has amazing plans for people, too. Invite a volunteer to read 1 Corinthians 2:9 from a Bible. **We don't understand everything that happens in our lives, just like we don't understand everything about hibernation. Things may even happen that we don't like. God can use those hard times to teach us things that will help us serve him better.**

Even though we don't fully understand how God works, we know he loves us. And just as God guides the chipmunks to wake up each spring, he'll guide us through the hard times of our lives. All we have to do is trust him!

Let's pray. Dear God, you do amazing things! You take care of the hibernating animals in your own special way. Help us to remember that you take care of us, too, even when we don't understand how. In Jesus' name, amen.

Down the Drain With Dirt

On Your Mark

Bible Truth: Jesus will forgive our sins when we ask him.

Bible Verse: Wash me. Then I will be whiter than snow. Let me hear you say, "Your sins are forgiven." Psalm 51:7–8

Godprint: Forgiveness

Get Set

You'll need a Bible, a bucket with clean water in it, and a small dirty doll or toy animal that will come clean when washed in the water.

GO!

It's the middle of winter! Sometimes in the middle of summer, I wish the weather would get cooler. Then in the winter time, like now, I wish the weather would get warmer! Wouldn't it be great if we could have snow in warm weather?

Let's pretend it's a really hot summer day. You've been playing outside all day. You've been running, jumping and sweating. It starts to get dark and it's time to come in. You're dirty and smelly. What do your parents say that you need? A bath!

I brought along a little pal of mine who was playing outside all day yesterday. He got sweaty and dirty and smelly. Look! Show the prop you brought. **This is my** (dog, Duke). **What do you think he needs? Yes, a bath. Well, I have a bucket of nice clean water here, so let's give him one.** Invite a couple of children to wash the prop in clean water. Be sure there is no dirt left before you show the rest of the children.

There! He looks great, doesn't he? Nice and clean. No more dirt. Let's think for a moment about how we get cleaned up when we're dirty.

• When you are all done with your bath, what happens to all the dirty water? (Right down the drain.)
• Can you get back the dirt that was on you?

Did you know that God washes the dirt off us that same way? And when God washes the dirt away, it's gone for good, too. Let's look at a Bible verse about that. Read key phrases from Psalm 51:7–8: Wash me. Then I will be whiter than snow. Let me hear you say, "Your sins are forgiven."

• When snow starts falling down from the sky and you catch it, what color is it? *(White.)*
• Is there any dirt on it? (No.)

The Bible says that when God washes us we'll be that white, that pure. Do you need God to wash you? I need God to wash me. We all need that from God. Every day as we're living life, we do things that hurt God. We say mean things or we don't tell the truth. Sometimes we think unkind thoughts about people. We might think of something nice to do for someone else, and be too busy or too lazy to do it. Or we might be so busy doing only what we want to do that we don't think about anybody else.

All those things hurt God and he calls that sin. Sin makes us feel dirty and sad on the inside. So God says, "Talk to me. Tell me you're sorry. I'll wash you so you're clean again."

• When we tell God we're sorry and he washes us white as snow, where does the sin go? *(Away for good.)*
• Can we get it back? *(No.)*

When God washes us, the sin is gone for good. He cleans us up and we are whiter than snow. We can have snow in the summer time after all!

Let's pray. Dear God, we're sorry that we do things that hurt you. We want you to wash us so clean that our hearts are white as snow. Please help us to keep our hearts clean. In Jesus' name, amen.

Tower Power

On Your Mark

Bible Truth: God wants us to work hard at the jobs he gives us to do.

Bible Verse: The plans of people who work hard succeed. You can be sure that those in a hurry will become poor. Proverbs 21:5.

Godprint: Diligence

Get Set

You'll need 50–100 plastic, colored cups, a Bible and a watch with a second hand.

GO!

Do we have any great builders in our group today? How many of you like to build with blocks or Legos®? Pause for a show of hands.

We're going to do some building today. See all of these cups? I want you to build a great tower. Make it as tall and as strong as you can. Oh, by the way, you only have 30 seconds. Ready, get set, Go!

If you have a lot of kids, you might want to have several groups working at the same time. Encourage the children to work as quickly as they can. At the end of 30 seconds, call time. The tower is likely to be either short and wide or tall and unstable.

Let's take a look at the tower you've built.

• Do you think this tower is strong and stable? Why not? *(It wobbles, it's too short to be a tower.)*
• Did you feel hurried to finish the tower? Why? *(We couldn't plan, we didn't have enough time, we had too many people putting cups on too fast.)*
• What do you think you could do to make a better tower? *(Talk to each other; plan; work together better.)*

Have you ever heard the story about the wise man and the foolish man? Jesus told that story. What do you remember about it? Pause to listen to what children can tell you about the story from Matthew 7:24–26.

The foolish man built his house on the sand because he was in a hurry. He wasn't careful, and he didn't have a good plan. But the wise man spent time finding a good solid place to build his house. When the storms came, the foolish man's house tumbled down.

If any part of the cup tower is still standing, pull one cup from the bottom of the tower and watch the tower fall down.

The wise man's house on the solid rock didn't fall when the wind and rain came. Let's read a verse from the Old Testament to help us understand why the wise man's house stayed up.

Have one child read Proverbs 21:5 from a Bible.

• What does this verse say is the key to success? (Working hard; plans.)
• What is one thing that can be hard about planning and hard work?

Now, I want you to build a new tower. Work together to make a plan and take your time putting the cups on top of each other. Let me see your very best work.

Give the children a couple of minutes to plan a strategy and build the cup tower.

Wow, now this is a great tower! By planning and working together you have succeeded just as God promised in Proverbs 21! Now let's all work together and put all the cups away.

Let's pray. Dear God, thank you for the work that you give us to do. Please help us remember to work hard and do a good job so that what we do for you will last. In Jesus' name, amen.

The Best Bait

On Your Mark

Bible Truth: God wants us to share the good news of Jesus.
Bible Verse: "Come. Follow me," Jesus said. "I will make you fishers of people." Matthew 4:19
Godprint: Evangelism

Get Set

You'll need a Bible and a tackle box with two chocolate hearts for each child.

GO!

Today we're going fishing. Right here in the church. I have everything we need to be good and successful fishermen. Hold up the tackle box with the chocolate hearts inside.

• What kinds of things would be in a tackle box to catch fish? *(Lures, bait, fishing line, hooks.)*
• Do you think it is possible for us to fish in church?

Obviously, we can't go fishing for fish in church. The church is on dry land, not in a pond. It would be silly to try to catch any fish in the church! So what do you think we might be fishing for today? Give the children a few seconds to guess.

Listen to this Bible verse and you will have a good idea. Have one child read Matthew 4:19 from a Bible. **We are going to fish for people! Did you know that was possible?**

• Why do you think Jesus would want us to fish for people? *(So they can know Jesus as we do—so we can all share the "Good News.")*
• How would fishing for people be like fishing for fish?
• What could we use to fish for people?
• What do you think is the best way to fish for people?

When you try to catch fish, you use things that the fish like. I have something in this tackle box that we can use to fish for people—something that people really want.

• What do you think I might have in this tackle box that we can use to fish for people?

After the children try to guess the contents, open the tackle box. Hold up the chocolate heart. **The best way to fish for people is with love**. Pass around the hearts. **When people see and feel God's love in you, they will want to know God, too. The best way to catch people for God is to show God's love to them.**

I have a chocolate heart for each of you to remind you that God loves you. Pass out one heart to each child. **But remember, today we are fishing for people. I have a second heart for you to use to fish for someone else**. Pass out a second heart to each child. **Share this heart with someone you love and you will be sharing the good news that God is love.**

Let's pray. Dear God, thank you for your love. Help us to show your love to the people around us so that they can know you, too. In Jesus' name, amen.

Optional: Extend this message by having the children pass out hearts to everyone in the congregation.

So High, So Low

On Your Mark

Bible Truth: God's love is beyond measure.

Bible Verse: May you have power with all God's people to understand Christ's love. May you know how wide and long and high and deep it is. And may you know his love, even though it can't be known completely. Then you will be filled with everything God has for you. Ephesians 3:18–19

Godprint: Worship

Get Set

You'll need your Bible, a pad of paper and pencil, a large empty box and a measuring tape or yard stick.

GO!

I have to mail something to a friend of mine. But I'm not sure if it will fit in this box. Maybe I'd better measure the box.

Place the box where the children can watch as you measure it. Have one of the older children write down the measurements as you call out how wide, long and high it is.

Thanks! I think it will work. Knowing the measurements helped a lot.

• Do you ever have to measure things?
• What kinds of things do you measure?
• How do you measure them?

We can measure our feet for shoes; we can measure furniture to see if it will fit in a room. We can measure the number of miles from one place to another. We can measure a floor for carpet. We can measure lots of things.

Is there anything we can't measure? What about the mountains? The oceans? The sky? Some of these things we can measure, some we can't. Let's see if you can guess some measurements. Use as many of the following examples as you have time for.

• Mount Everest is the tallest mountain in the world. How tall do you think it is? *(29,028 feet.)*

• Olympus Mons is a mountain on Mars. How high do you think it is? *(Fifteen miles high, three times higher than Mount Everest on earth, and at the top it is 45 miles across!)*

• How deep is the ocean? *(The average depth of the ocean is 2.5 miles. The deepest point lies in the Mariana Trench, 6.8 miles down. That's deeper than Mount Everest is high!)*

• How deep is a cave? *(The deepest natural caves that people know about are the Pierre St. Martin Caves in the Pyrenees Mountains between Spain and France, which reach 4,370 feet deep. That's almost three times as deep as the Empire State Building is high!)*

• How far away from the earth is the moon? *(240,000 miles.)* How about the sun? *(93 million miles.)*

Even though it is possible to measure how high a mountain is or how deep a sea is, the measurements are amounts so great that we can't understand them. The highest mountain, the deepest sea, the widest distance in space—all were made by God. And he has the wisdom and power to know their measure.

In Ephesians, the Apostle Paul prays that we would have the power to know something so high, so deep, so wide that it is impossible to measure. Read Ephesians 3:18 from a Bible or ask a confident reader to do it.

God wants you to know that he loves you so much that you can't even understand how deep, how wide, how high his love is for you. Can you imagine a love so big? I know I can't! But every day as I read my Bible and pray and learn more about God, I understand his love a little more. It makes me want to praise and worship him. Let's praise him together. Sing a chorus, offer applause to God, or lead in another form of praise appropriate for your group.

Let's pray. Dear Father, your love for us is so big that we can't understand it, but we know it's true. We worship you and thank you for loving us with such a big love. In Jesus' name, amen.

What's Undercover Counts

On Your Mark

Bible Truth: God looks at what is inside our hearts.

Bible Verse: But the LORD said to Samuel, "Do not consider how handsome or tall he is. I have not chosen him. I do not look at the things people look at. Man looks at how someone appears on the outside. But I look at what is in the heart." 1 Samuel 16:7

Godprint: Integrity

Get Set

You'll need your Bible, some yucky trash, a shoebox or other medium-sized box, and some gift wrap, tape and ribbon. Put some trash in the box and wrap it as beautifully as you can. You'll also need a white cloth big enough to cover the box.

GO!

Come in close! I want to tell you a story this morning. A little boy named Bobby had a bedroom with a window in it and when Bobby looked outside his window, he could see his large front yard.

One winter night Bobby's big sister told him to peek outside his window to see a surprise. Bobby scrambled to the window. He saw tiny snowflakes falling from the sky. The first snow of the winter was coming! Bobby was excited about the snow, but that lasted for only a moment. Something else caught Bobby's attention. All over his front yard he saw trash. Earlier the wind had been blowing. It blew over a neighbor's trash can and the trash was all over Bobby's yard. Right away Bobby decided that when morning came, he would clean up that trash all by himself.

When morning came and Bobby woke up, he remembered the job he could do all by himself. He ran to the window. He could not believe his eyes. The trash was all gone and in its place was snow, snow, snow! The snow completely covered his bushes and was so deep it was half way up his fence. The yard looked wonderful. "There's no trash to clean up now," Bobby thought.

Isn't it nice when a big mess just goes away and you don't have to clean it up? It's much nicer to look at pretty things. Show the children the gift wrapped box. **This box certainly is beautiful. I wonder what is inside. Can you guess?** Let the children share any possibilities they can imagine as to the contents of the box. Encourage ideas that seem to be consistent with the beautiful wrapping on the box. **Let's take a look.** Invite a child to tear off the wrapping paper. Remove the lid from the shoe box and excitedly look inside without revealing to the children the contents. **Oh, my! This is a surprise. The box was so beautiful on the outside but the inside is…well, yucky! Take a look! This looks like the trash from Bobby's yard!** Reveal the contents of the box to the children. Expect exclamations of surprise and disgust.

Well, we can't put the wrapping paper back on. Mmm. I know! We'll cover it up, just like the snow covered the trash in Bobby's yard. Place the white cloth over the trash. **There, now doesn't that look beautiful again? Raise your hand if you think the trash is still there.**

Remove the cloth and show the trash. **You're right! Bobby was tricked by the snow, but you weren't tricked at all.**

This reminds me of a story in the Bible. King Saul was tall and handsome on the outside, but in his heart he disobeyed God. When God decided to choose a new king for Israel, the prophet Samuel was looking for a man who was handsome and tall. Read 1 Samuel 16:7 or have a confident reader do it.

• Does God care about your clothes or hair or shoes?

Remember, God counts what is in the heart of each person as most important. When God looks at us, it's who we are on the inside that counts. And God helps us keep our hearts clean so we're just as nice on the inside as we look on the outside.

Let's pray. Dear Jesus, we know that sometimes we try to look good on the outside when we have trash on the inside. Please help us to clean up our trash and clean up our hearts. Thank you for helping us. In Jesus' name, amen.

Snow Angels

On Your Mark

Bible Truth: God makes each of us different from anyone else.

Bible Verse: You created the deepest parts of my being. You put me together inside my mother's body. How you made me is amazing and wonderful. I praise you for that. What you have done is wonderful. I know that very well. Psalm 139:13–14

Godprint: Preciousness

Get Set

You'll need a variety of paper snowflakes cut from white paper and placed in a paper bag. Try not to make any two exactly alike. Make enough for each child to have one. You'll also need a Bible. Optional: invite children to cut their own snowflakes.

GO!

Have you ever looked very closely at a snowflake? Did you know that every single snowflake that falls is different than all the others? Each one has a different design or pattern. The differences can be very tiny because the snowflakes are so small, but they are there. I have some bigger snowflakes for you to look at. See if you can find some different patterns in these snowflakes. Hand each child a paper snowflake and give children a minute to compare them with their neighbors'. **See if you can find someone who has a snowflake exactly like yours.**

• Did you find any differences in the snowflakes?
• How are the snowflakes the same?

Ask the children to stand in a big circle. **Look around at your friends in this circle. Go stand next to someone who has the same hair color as you.** Pause and let children regroup. Help some of the younger ones find the right group if necessary.

Now find someone who has the same hair color _and_ the same eye color as you. Pause to regroup again. Children will have more trouble finding someone alike.

Now how about someone with the same hair color, same eye color _and_ the same face as you. Pause again. Unless you have identical twins in your group, no one will be able to find someone with the same face! Ask the children to sit down again.

Did you find someone who looks exactly like you? Not just someone with the same color eyes or same color hair. I mean someone who looks like you in a mirror. Did you find someone? No? Even twins have some differences in the way they look or act. Every single person on this planet is just like a snowflake. No two people are exactly alike, just as no two snowflakes are the same.

When God made each of you, he planned the way you would be right down to your freckles and smiles. He made each of you in a special and wonderful way. We can read it right here in the Book of Psalms.

Choose a good reader to read Psalm 139:13–14 from a Bible.

People are all unique and marvelous beings created by God. God made each of us in his image but he also made each of us to be our own person. We all have our own thoughts and ideas, our own looks and personalities. As different as we all are, God loves each of us just the same.

Take your snowflake home with you. Find a special place to hang it and every time you see it, remember that God himself made you just the way he wanted you. You are special and unique to God and he loves you.

Be sure to have plenty of snowflakes on hand so no child will be left out. If you want, hand each child a second snowflake to give to someone in the congregation.

Let's pray. Dear God, you are amazing and wonderful. Thank you for making us and loving us. No one else can do what you do. We praise you. In Jesus' name, amen.

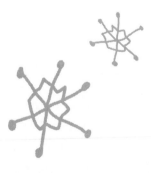

Surprised By Joy

On Your Mark

Bible Truth: God's love gives me joy.

Bible Verse: The LORD gives me strength. He is like a shield that keeps me safe. My heart trusts in him and he helps me. My heart jumps for joy. I will sing and give thanks to him. Psalm 28:7

Godprint: Joy

Get Set

You'll need a Bible, a box of valentines, a marker and a large red poster board heart. Cut two parallel vertical slits near the center of the heart to create a handle. You'll also need a colored construction paper heart for each child. If possible, cut these hearts out of many different colors of construction paper.

GO!

Valentine's Day is coming up, and I have a few valentine questions for you.

• How many of you will be giving out valentines?
• Do you give them to everyone, or just certain special people?
• How do you feel when someone you care about gives you a valentine?
• How do you feel when you don't receive a valentine from that special someone?

Hold up the box of valentines. **I have a box of valentines here. Let's open it and take a look inside.** Let children help you open the box, then take out a few of the cards. Read some of the greetings. Continue reading until you begin to read duplicates.

Now, wait a minute. We already read one like that. Sometimes valentines can be so predictable. They always say the same thing: "Be my valentine," or something like that. The pictures and characters are different, but the message is exactly the same. This Valentine's Day, let's create a valentine that will really surprise people.

Take out the large red heart and marker. **This is the biggest valentine I could make, and it's from the person who loves us most of all. Can anyone guess who it's from? That's right,** it's a valentine from God. Let's see what we know about God's love. We can write our ideas right on the valentine.

Let children respond. Write their ideas on the large heart. **Wow. What a great valentine. This is much better than those boxed cards or even those valentine candy hearts. I've got one more thing to add about God's love.**

Write "KEEPS US SAFE" on the heart.

Did you know God's love keeps us safe? Read the first part of Psalm 28:7 from a Bible: "The Lord gives me strength. He is like a shield that keeps me safe. My heart trusts in him and he helps me." Stop before "My heart jumps for joy."

Feeling safe is a good feeling, isn't it? We feel safe when we're loved. We know the people who love us will take care of us, provide for our needs, and protect us from scary things that may come along. God does all that for us and more. That's a valentine we can really be glad about!

Grab the handle in the center of the red heart and hold it up. God's love gives us joy. If you want to put your trust in God and accept his valentine, come join me behind this heart-shield.

Wait for the children to join you, then quickly give each child a colored heart. Quietly give them the instructions to jump up and toss their colored hearts in the air when they hear the word "joy." Keep this process a secret from the adult audience as much as possible.

Now that we're all safe and secure behind the shield of God's love, let's hear the rest of our Bible verse. I got so excited about God's love I think I stopped reading before the end. Now, where was I? Oh, maybe I'll just read the whole thing again.

Motion to the children to get ready, then read Psalm 28:7. Pause briefly after you read each phrase. When you read the phrase, "My heart jumps for joy," have the children jump up and throw their hearts.

Let's pray. Dear Lord, thank you for the shield of your love to keep us safe. Thank you that our hearts can jump for joy because you keep us safe. In Jesus' name, amen.

You're Invited

winter

On Your Mark

Bible Truth: God wants to live in our hearts.

Bible Verse: "Here I am! I stand at the door and knock. If any of you hears my voice and opens the door, I will come in and eat with you. And you will eat with me." Revelation 3:20.

Godprint: Commitment

Get Set

You'll need a party invitation with an RSVP card and small map. Make copies of the invitation on page 58 on bright colored paper. You'll also need a Bible.

GO!

I brought something with me to share with you today. It's an invitation to a party. Hold up the invitation for children to see, then pass it around the circle for children to investigate.

• What information can we find out from this invitation? *(When the party is, where it will be, who is giving the party, what the party is celebrating.)*
• Have you ever gotten a party invitation?
• How did you feel when someone wanted you to come and share a fun day?
• What's your favorite thing to eat at a party?

This invitation has some other things with it. Hold up the RSVP card. **The host of the party would like to know who is coming. I can send this little card back to the person having the party to say, "Yes, I am coming!"** Pass the RSVP card around. **When I send this card back, I am promising to come to the party. I have made a commitment to come to the party. Now my friend who is giving the party is expecting me.**

• Have you ever had someone say "Yes, I am coming to the party" and then not come?
• How did that make you feel?

Jesus has invited us all to a party. The party celebrates God's love for us. Open the Bible to Revelation 3:20 and ask one child to read the verse.

Jesus comes to each of our hearts and invites us to the party. He wants to come into our hearts so we can enjoy being with him. He asks each of us to say, "Yes, I am coming to the party." If we say, "Yes, please come in," we make a commitment to him, just like when we say "yes" on the RSVP card.

Sometimes people might say "yes" on the card, but they get lost on the way to the party. This invitation I have has a little map in it so I won't get lost on my way to the party. Pass the map around the circle.

God has given us a "map" to his party too. Do you know what the map is? That's right, the Bible. God knows that sometimes it might be hard to keep our commitment to him. It might be because we are having hard times or we get really busy. But with the Bible, we can always find our way back to God.

I have something for you. Pass out the invitations.

• What is this invitation for? (A party with Jesus.)
• Where is the party? (In our hearts.)
• When is the party? (Starting right now.)

It's up to you to accept the invitation and make a commitment to go to the party with Jesus. Don't forget to celebrate!

Let's pray. Dear Jesus, thank you for inviting us to your party. Thank you that you want to be with us. Help us to accept your invitation and open our hearts so you can come in for the party. In your name, amen.

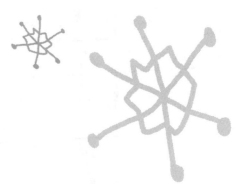

What: Party with Jesus
Where: In our hearts
When: Starting right now.

What: Party with Jesus
Where: In our hearts
When: Starting right now.

What: Party with Jesus
Where: In our hearts
When: Starting right now.

What: Party with Jesus
Where: In our hearts
When: Starting right now.

Take a Shower Every Day!

On Your Mark

Bible Truth: God's Word causes us to grow spiritually.

Bible Verse: The rain and the snow come down from the sky. They do not return to it without watering the earth. They make plants come up and grow. The plants produce seeds for farmers. They also produce food for people to eat. The words I speak are like that. They will not return to me without producing results. They will accomplish what I want them to. They will do exactly what I sent them to do. Isaiah 55:10–11

Godprint: Discipleship

Get Set

You'll need a Bible, a plant in a small pot, a small pot with only dirt, and a squirt bottle with water.

GO!

Have you ever heard the rhyme, "April showers bring May flowers?" Begin to lightly squirt the children with water as you explain. **What helps flowers to grow?** Repeat the rhyme, emphasizing "showers." **Right! Showers. But wait a minute; you don't put your plants in the tub, do you? No! Plants don't take showers. But what kind of water helps plants to grow? Rain! Yes! Look at this pot.** Show the pot of dirt. **What's inside?** (Dirt.)

Hidden under the dirt is a seed. God knows that the plants hidden under the ground need water to grow, so he sends rain. After a little while something starts to grow and poke up through the dirt and pretty soon, what do you see? Show the potted plant.

Has anyone ever been lying in bed listening or watching the rain outside a window? What does it sound like? (Pitter patter, soft, hard.) **The rain falling means God is watering the earth so plants can grow. Well, just like we listen to the rain and know something is going to grow outside, listening to God will make us grow inside. Let's see what God says in the Book of Isaiah, chapter 55, verses 10-11.** Read the verses from a Bible or ask a confident child to read.

God says the words he speaks are like rain and snow, watering the plants.

Spring

• How do we hear God speak? *(By reading what God says in the Bible.)*

Hold up your Bible. **This book is God's Word. In Isaiah, God says if we listen to his Word, good things will happen inside us. We'll begin to grow, just like these plants.** Show both pots and point accordingly. **One pot has just dirt and the seed is buried. The other has a beautiful plant that can make more seeds and feed people and make people happy because it's so pretty to see.**

•Which is more useful? *(The one that's growing.)*
• How many of you want to grow?

Let me tell you the secret for growing. Is everyone listening? Huddle down with the children as if you're going to whisper a big secret. **If you want to grow, take a shower every day! Not this kind of shower** *(lightly squirt the children),* **but shower yourselves with this.** Show the Bible.

When you hear the rain outside, you know the plants are getting what they need to grow. When you hear God's Word and listen to it, you are getting what you need to grow on the inside.

So, what do we do to grow? *(Show the Bible.)* **Take a shower every day!**

Let's pray. Lord, shower us with your Word every day. Water us and make us grow. Please help us to grow into disciples who do exactly what you want us to do. In Jesus' name, amen.

Rock-a-Bye Baby

On Your Mark

Bible Truth: God loves us and cares for us like a loving parent.

Bible Verse: The LORD your God is with you. He is mighty enough to save you. He will take great delight in you. The quietness of his love will calm you down. He will sing with joy because of you. Zephaniah 3:17

Godprint: Preciousness

Get Set

You'll need a Bible and a young baby. Invite a mother or father with a new baby to help you by bringing the baby to the front and singing a lullaby.

GO!

We have a special guest with us this morning. Introduce the baby and parents. *(Baby's name)*'**s mommy and daddy have to work really hard to take care of a baby. I'm sure a lot of you have been around babies, and you know what it takes.**

• What are some things parents do to take care of a baby? *(Allow a few volunteers to share their ideas.)*

Wow! That is a lot of hard work! And they have to do this all the time. Lots of times they even have to get up in the middle of the night. And sometimes the things they have to do are pretty yucky!

• Why in the world do mommies and daddies do all those things? *(Wait for response from the kids.)*

Parents do all these things because they love their babies. *(Dad's name)* **and** *(Mom's name)* **want** *(baby's name)* **to know that** *(he or she)* **is safe and cared for. Anyone can change a baby's diaper or feed a baby. But mommies and daddies do special things to show their babies just how precious they are.**

• What are some ways that your moms and dads show how much they love you? What special things do they do?

Sometimes mommies and daddies show love to their babies by tickling their toes and kissing their tummies. Sometimes they rock them to sleep and sing them lullabies.

Invite Mom and Dad to sing a lullaby to their baby for the children. Then thank the parents and let them return to their seats.

Do you know that God loves you just like this mommy and daddy love their baby? You are so precious to him that he is always with you and even sings happy songs to you.

Read Zephaniah 3:17 from a Bible or ask a good reader to do it.

Isn't that amazing? The God who made the whole world delights in you! That means he is proud of you, and when he watches you pray and sing his praises, it makes him happy. When you are sad or afraid, he is with you and will help you feel safe again.

• How does God's love calm you down?
• If we could hear the words of God's song, what do you think the song would say?

Sometimes when babies cry, no one can calm them down except Mommy or Daddy. Other people may try, but Mom and Dad just have a special touch. You know, it's like that with God, too. Sometimes things happen to us, and, while the people around us can love us and encourage us, the only way we ever really feel better is when we remember to go to God. I want you to remember how precious you are to God. Remember that he sings joyful songs over you and is just waiting to calm you with his love

Let's pray. Dear Lord, thank you for being mighty. Thank you for taking delight in us. Help us to remember that your love calms us down. In Jesus' name, amen.

Tongue Twister

On Your Mark

Bible Truth: God wants us to use our tongues to be kind to others.

Bible Verse: Have a pure and loving heart, and speak kindly. Then you will be a friend of the king. Proverbs 22:11

Godprint: Kindness

Get Set

You'll need a Bible and lunch bag puppets with eyes and a mouth drawn on each. Each child will need a puppet.

GO!

Who likes to go to the movies? Listen to all the excited responses.

Did you know that many years ago there were movies that had no talking at all? Well, the actors "talked" but you couldn't hear them. Their tongues wiggled but no sound came out of their mouths. These movies were called "silent movies," and the audience had to read the words on the big silver screen to know what was going on. Let's have our very own silent movie now!

Distribute the lunch bag puppets. Ask kids to put their hands inside.

Each of you has your own movie S.T.A.R. (Silent, Talented And Responsive) puppet! Open and close your hand to give the puppet's mouth a try! Pause. **Now when I give a thumbs up, I'd like each of your puppets to "talk" to your neighbor but not to make a sound. Go ahead and give it a try.** Give a thumbs-up sign. After awhile say, **Hmm. Silence really *is* golden!**

Now when I give you a thumbs-down your puppets are to stop being silent movie stars and talk out loud. Ready to give it a try? Give a thumbs-down sign. Kids will suddenly begin to chatter very loudly! **Good!**

Now everyone watch me very carefully and be ready to respond. Switch slowly between the thumbs-up and thumbs-down signal. Finally, keep one thumb up but flip the other one down! The sudden confusion will leave your kids babbling, much to the delight of your congregation!

Hmm. It seems that we had a little trouble controlling our tongues. I think I even saw one or two children completely tongue-tied! Ask kids to remove their S.T.A.R. puppets and place them in their laps.

Yes, sirree. Our tongues can lead us into trouble. Hurtful words hurt! We also hurt others when we tell lies, small or big ones.

Read Proverbs 22:11 from a Bible or ask an older child to read the verse.

• How can your "tongue" get you into trouble at school?
• How can you hurt another person with the words that you say?
• How can you treat someone kindly by what you say?

Ask kids to slip on their puppets again. **Treat others with kindness in everything you say and do, just as Jesus did. That's how you can show you're a friend of King Jesus!**

Let's pray. Jesus, we want to use our tongues to show that we have loving hearts. Help us to treat each other with kindness. In Jesus' name, amen.

While you have children huddled and quiet for prayer, whisper that as they return to their seats they may wave their puppets and shout, "We can be kind to others. How about you?" Count to three to get everyone started.

Important King, Important Thing

On Your Mark

Bible Truth: Following God is the most important thing we can do.

Bible Verse: And why do you worry about clothes? See how the wild flowers grow. They don't work or make clothing. But here is what I tell you. Not even Solomon in all of his glory was dressed like one of those flowers...Put God's kingdom first. Do what he wants you to do. Then all of those things will also be given to you. Matthew 6:28–29, 33.

Godprint: Commitment

Get Set

You'll need a Bible, dress-up clothing for a king (including a crown), and a lily or other flower sticker for each child.

GO!

Have you ever imagined that you were a king or queen? Kings and queens are really important people, aren't they?

• What would you do if you were a king or queen?
• What would you wear if you were a king or queen?

The Bible tells us about a lot of kings. King Saul was the very first king of God's people. He was a strong warrior. King David was Israel's next king. David loved God and tried his best to follow him. David had a son named Solomon, and Solomon became king after David. Solomon built a beautiful temple where people could go to worship God. Solomon had palaces and servants. He wore fancy clothes and had lots of beautiful things. People from all over came to visit Solomon, and they all told him what an important king he was.

Let's pretend for a minute that I'm an important king like King Solomon. Can you help me put on these royal clothes so I can look kingly?

Distribute the dress-up items. Have children work together to dress you up. End by having someone "crown" you as king.

Oh, I feel so kingly and important. Now that I'm the king, I can tell everyone what to do.

Point to different children as you give the following commands:

• You, stand up.
• You, lie down.
• You, bring me my royal breakfast.
• You, admire my royal crown. How many jewels are in it?
• You and you, trade places, please. You're blocking my royal view.
• Excuse me, but could I please have that seat? I am the king, so that makes me more important.

Take off your crown.

• Am I acting like a king?
• Am I acting like a *good, kind* king?
• What's the most important thing a king should do?

Whether we're kings and queens or regular people, following God is the most important thing we can do. For a while Solomon was a good and wise king, but as time went by he got more and more anxious to impress the people who came to his palace. He forgot about following God and spent all his time trying to impress people with his beautiful things. At the end of his life most of his kingdom was taken away because he'd disobeyed God.

Solomon was a great and powerful king. Jesus had something to say about King Solomon. Read Matthew 6:28–29, 33 from a Bible.

• How important were all the beautiful things Solomon had?
• How are the flowers of the field more beautiful than Solomon?
• Do the flowers have to do anything to be beautiful?

When we choose to follow God we do things God's way, not our own way. We don't have to try to impress other people the way Solomon did. We can stop worrying about how cool we are or how much stuff we have. Because if we're following God, he'll make sure we have what we need, just like he takes care of the flowers.

Speaking of Solomon (put your crown back on), **I have one last royal request.** Hold up the flower stickers. **Would everyone please pick a flower from my royal garden? Put your flower on your chest, over your heart, to remind you to love and follow God this week.**

Let's pray. God our king, thank you for making the beautiful wild flowers grow. Help us to remember that if we follow you, you will take care of us the way you take care of the flowers. Amen.

Star Light, Star Bright

On Your Mark

Bible Truth: God wants us to be a light in a world dark with sin.

Bible Verse: Do everything without finding fault or arguing. Then you will be pure and without blame. You will be children of God without fault in a sinful and evil world. Among the people of the world you shine like stars in the heavens. Philippians: 2:14–15

Godprint: Commitment

Get Set

You'll need your Bible, a handheld mirror, and a flashlight with fresh batteries. You can use a mirror with a non-glass back side that does not reflect, or paint the magnified side of a two-sided mirror with black tempera paint ahead of time. Optional: a glow-in-the dark star for each child. Before your talk, paint the magnified side of the mirror with the black paint and let dry.

GO!

Hold up the glass side of the mirror for the kids to see and ask:

• What's this I'm holding? *(A mirror.)*
• What does a mirror do? *(Shows us what we look like; reflects things.)*

Walk up to several children and let them look into the mirror as you hold it. Ask them what they see. **Does anyone know how a mirror works?** Some of your older kids may be able to share the concept that light goes into the mirror, hits the back surface and reflects the image back. Emphasize that the mirror needs light going into it in order to reflect an image we can see.

Turn the mirror around with the non-glass (or painted) side out.

• Now, what do you see? *(Nothing. The light is not reaching the mirrored side.)*

Turn the flashlight on and shine it on the back side of the mirror.

• **Does this help?** *(No. The mirror still can't reflect the light.)*
Without the light hitting the mirror's surface, it can't reflect or show back anything.

Read Philippians 2:14–15 from a Bible. **God has asked us to be like a mirror—reflecting his light and love to the world. But when we focus on each other's faults and argue with each other, it's like we have something dark over our mirrors and we can't reflect his light.**

If possible, dim the lights in the room as you say, **We live in a world that is dark with sin. People around us need the light of Jesus.** Turn the flashlight on and hold it close to the glass side of the mirror so that the light reflects on the ceiling or wall where the kids can see it. **When our lives are clean and pure, God's light shines out from us. God has called us to shine like stars in a dark world. When the world sees our light, they will want to know and follow Jesus.**

Turn the lights back up. **You are never too young or too old to be like a star shining God's light to those around you. Would you like to be a star for Jesus?** Pass out a star to each child. **This star will remind you this week to keep from finding fault in others and from arguing. It will remind you to be a light to the world.**

Let's pray. Father of Light, we want to show your love to the world around us. Help us to live lives that shine like lights in the darkness. In Jesus' name, amen.

Suckers

On Your Mark

Bible Truth: God wants to us focus on things that build his kingdom.
Bible Verse: Put everything to the test. Hold on to what is good. 1 Thessalonians 5:21
Godprint: Wisdom

Get Set

You'll need a Bible and large paper grocery bags. In one, place enough lollipops for each child to have one. (If you're feeling really generous, pack enough lollipops for the entire congregation!) In the other, place three stalks of weeds you've pulled up and labeled, *TV, video games, talking on the phone.*

GO!

• Who can tell me what a sucker is?

Aha! You're all thinking of *this* kind of sucker. Pass the bag of lollipops around and let kids enjoy the treat as you continue the devotion. But I'm thinking of a *different* kind of sucker entirely.

• Does anyone know anything about different kinds of suckers?

The suckers I'm thinking of grow at the base of trees. There's the nice, thick main trunk. But then, lots of trees put out skinny little shoots around the trunk every spring. They don't look very nice. They make the tree look kind of raggedy. And they're a real pain because you can't just wait until a nice soft rain and then pull them out. They are really attached— right down to the root of the tree. And if you don't cut them out, they'll grow tall and pull the nourishment and water away from the main part of the tree.

Sometimes the things we like to do become suckers in our lives. I'll show you what I mean.

Hand the second bag to someone, have him or her pull out a weed and read the label.

• How does (watching TV, playing video games, chatting on the phone) suck time away from more important things?

• How would your life be different if you trimmed back those suckers?

• Do you think kids are the only ones who have problems with suckers? Why or why not?

As children of God—both adults and kids—there's one thing we all need to do that's more important than anything else, and that's use our energy and talent and imagination to build up God's kingdom. Listen to what Paul says about that. Read 1 Thessalonians 5:21 from a Bible.

• When it says "Test everything," does that mean like the tests your teachers give you at school? What does it mean?

• How can you hold on to what's good and work for God's kingdom?

This week when you go home from church, I hope you'll remember to hold on to what's good—to what builds up God's kingdom—and trim back the suckers that are pulling time and energy from the really important things in your life. If you're ready to do that, wave your lollipop in the air. Great! I'll be praying for you!

Optional: If you have suckers for the entire congregation, let the kids pass them out as they return to their seats. These lollipops will remind all the adult children of God to do the same thing.

Let's pray. Dear God, you are good and wise. Help us to not to let things that aren't important take away from things that are important. Help us to make wise choices. In Jesus' name, amen.

A Clean Slate

On Your Mark

Bible Truth: To be forgiven, all we have to do is ask.

Bible Verse: But God is faithful and fair. If we admit that we have sinned, he will forgive us our sins. He will forgive every wrong thing we have done. He will make us pure. 1 John 1:9

Godprint: Forgiveness

Get Set

You'll need colored chalk for each child, pre-moistened towelettes and a Bible.

GO!

• Who can tell us what a slate is?

Slate is an old-fashioned word for chalkboard. Long ago, chalkboards were made of a kind of rock called slate. At school, the children had slates to hold in their hands. Instead of using paper and pencils, children would write on their slates.

Let's pretend our hands are like a slate. Draw a sad face on your palm. Give each child a piece of chalk. **Now draw a sad face on your slate.**

Uh, oh. I goofed. I don't want to be sad, but I have a sad face on my hand. What can I do about it? Wait for children to suggest wiping it off. Rub your hands together briskly to remove the chalk. Encourage the kids to do the same thing. Hold up your clean hands and ask the children to hold up theirs.

Now we have a "clean slate." We can start all over again. When the teacher was ready to teach a new lesson, she would tell the students it was time to wipe their slates clean. In other words, it was time to start over, just the way we did.

When we mess up and do something that makes God sad, God helps us wipe our slates clean and start over too. It's very easy. The Bible tells us exactly how to do it. Ask a good reader to read 1 John 1:9 from a Bible.

• What does this verse say we should do when we do something wrong? *(Admit it.)*
• What does God do when we admit our wrong? *(Forgives us.)*

When we make bad choices or do things that we know are wrong, God is sad. When we sin, we're not close to God, and God wants us to be close to him all the time. He doesn't ever want us to be away from him.

God gave us a way to come back close to him when we mess up. All we have to do is ask God to forgive us. That's it! Once our slate has been wiped clean, God will bring us back close to him. Then not only is God happy again, but so are we.

Let's draw happy faces on our slates. Draw a happy face on your palm and encourage the kids to do the same.

Making good choices and trying to live our lives the way God wants us to may seem hard sometimes. But isn't it great to know that God has made it so easy to fix those messes and stay close to him? And remember, you can wipe the mess away any time you want. God always forgives when we admit our messes. Sometimes at this time of year, we think about "spring cleaning" for our houses. Let's also think about cleaning our hearts.

I am going to say a prayer right now. If you need to have your slate wiped clean, ask God to forgive you while I pray.

Dear God, thank you for thinking up the great idea of forgiveness. We are glad that you want us to be close to you all the time. Help us remember that we can wipe our slates clean anytime we need to. All we need to do is ask. In Jesus' name, amen.

Read the Map

On Your Mark

Bible Truth: God wants us to follow the paths that he shows us.

Bible Verses: Make level paths for your feet to walk on. Only go on ways that are firm. Don't turn to the right or left. Keep your feet from the path of evil. Proverbs 4:26–27

Your word is like a lamp that shows me the way. It is like a light that guides me. Psalm 119:105.

Godprint: Hope

Get Set

You'll need a Bible and a map. On the map use brightly colored highlighters to highlight a straight road and one that is very hilly and windy with many switchbacks. The routes you mark do not have to be real roads.

GO!

I need your help. I'm thinking about planning a trip. I'd like to go on a hike on a great trail I heard about. But I have one problem. I don't know how to get there.

• What should I do if I'm going to take a trip and I don't know the way? *(Let children answer.)*

Pull out your map. **Someone gave me this map.**

• How could this help me? *(Give you directions; keep you from getting lost; show you the best road to take.)*

Wow! A map can do all that? What a great guide! I'm definitely going to use it! It can tell me a lot of important information.

• Who thinks it is important to know where you are going?
• Who thinks it's important not to get lost?

If you do get lost, a map can show you where you made a wrong turn and how to get back on the right path. Look what else this map shows me. It shows the best path to take. Show the map and point to the straight line.

If I follow this road I can stay on one path. I don't have to make a lot of turns. This is a nice straight road. If I follow it, I won't get into trouble. It would be hard to get lost. But look at this path. Point to the curvy line. **If I go this way it looks pretty dangerous. I could get hurt or hurt someone else going this direction. I could get lost and not know which way to turn.**

• If you were going on a trip, which path would you take?

Surprise! You *are* **going on a trip. All of us are. God has a special trip planned for each one of us. God calls that trip "his purposes for us." He has a straight path that he wants us to follow. He doesn't want us to take the wrong way and get hurt or hurt others or get lost. He wants to show us the best way to go, the safest, happiest, best path for us.**

• What do you think God gave us to use as our map? *(The Bible.)*

Listen to what God says in Psalm 119:105. Read the verse from a Bible. **I hope you're thinking, "Wow! The Bible can do all that? What a great guide! I'm definitely going to use it!"**

Now let's read some verses that make us think of a map. Read Proverbs 4:26–27. Read the verses from a Bible or invite a confident reader to do it. **God wants us to use this map** (show your Bible) **every day. The Bible helps us to know what the best path is, so we won't turn to the right or to the left when we're not supposed to.**

Turn to the congregation and hold your Bible up in the air. **If you have one of these maps today, hold it up!** Pause. **Wow! A lot of people have the right map! We can help each other not get lost.**

The Bible is our map. Use it everyday to stay on the right path and please God.

Let's pray. Dear Lord, thank you for giving us a map to show us how to go where you want us to go. Help us to read the map and keep from getting lost. In Jesus' name, amen.

Hip, Hip Hooray for Mom

On Your Mark

Bible Truth: God wants us to respect our mothers.

Bible Verse: She speaks wisely. She teaches faithfully. She watches over family matters. She is busy all the time. Her children stand up and call her blessed. Her husband also rises up, and he praises her. He says, "Many women do noble things. But you are better than all the others." Charm can fool you. Beauty fades. But a woman who has respect for the LORD should be praised. Give her the reward she has earned. Proverbs 31:26–31

Godprint: Respectfulness

Get Set

You'll need your Bible. Optional: paper megaphones, noisemakers

GO!

• What things make you feel like cheering? *(Take a few responses.)*

Do you feel like cheering? When I give the signal, everyone stand up and give your best cheer. You can stomp, clap or call out. When I give the second signal, then we'll stop cheering. Ready? Give a hand signal or use a noisemaker. After a few seconds of cheering, give the signal to stop.

Today we're all going to celebrate someone special, someone who deserves our thanks and praise. Today we are going to celebrate moms. In Proverbs 31, we read about a special woman—one who honored God and her family. If you think about it, you might find that you have a mom like the woman in Proverbs 31. Let's take a look.

Open your Bible and read from Proverbs 31 one phrase at a time and give the following comments:

She speaks wisely (v. 26).
Have you ever noticed that your mom knows a lot of stuff? She answers your questions and gives good advice. If you have a mom like that, stand up and cheer. Give the signal for children to stand up and cheer.

She teaches faithfully (v. 26).
Your mom doesn't have to work in a classroom to be a teacher. In fact, during your life so far you have probably learned more from your mom than any other one person. Moms teach us about a lot of things every day, even when they're tired. Stand up and cheer if your mom teaches you. Give the signals to start and stop.

She watches over family matters (v. 27).
Moms have a lot of responsibility at home. They keep things running smoothly and take care of everyone in the family. Does your mom take care of things at home? Stand up and cheer. Give the signals to start and stop.

She is busy all the time (v. 27).
I don't think I've ever met a mom who wasn't busy! Whether your mom works at home or has a job away from home, you have probably noticed that she is busy all the time. Busy moms deserve a cheer. Let's stand up and cheer for busy moms. Give the signals to start and stop.

Her children stand up and call her blessed (v. 28).
Blessing someone can be a way of saying "thank you." If your mom is here, stand up, point to her and say, "Thank you!"

Okay, dads. Now it's your turn. Proverbs 31:28–29 says "Her husband also rises up, and he praises her. He says, 'Many women do noble things. But you are better than all the others.'" So dads, stand up, look at your wife and tell her she is the best! You may have to do a little coaxing, but it's important for the children to see their dads honoring their moms too.

Great job, everyone. Our Bible passage today ends with a reminder. It says that charm and beauty don't last. That's not what is important. But a woman who loves God and follows him deserves to be praised—not just today but every day. So, let's give all our moms one last cheer! Give the signals.

Let's pray. Dear Father, thank you for the mothers that you gave us. Help us to learn from them and honor them the way you want us to. Remind us to show our moms the respect they deserve. In Jesus' name, amen.

Holy Spirit Power!

On Your Mark

Bible Truth: God gives me the power to follow him.

Bible Verse: But you will receive power when the Holy Spirit comes on you. Then you will be my witnesses in Jerusalem. You will be my witnesses in all Judea and Samaria. And you will be my witnesses from one end of the earth to the other. Acts 1:8

Godprint: Conviction

Get Set

You'll need a Bible, a water-based marker and one or more superhero costume items, such as mask, cape, belt or boots.

GO!

• Who's your favorite superhero?
• What makes superheroes so super?

Superheroes are "super" because they're good guys. They're always on the lookout for trouble, and when they find it, they put a stop to it. They catch the bad guys and stop them from doing bad things.

I've brought some things that superheroes sometimes wear. You can help me put them on. We'll talk a little bit about each one, and when I've got them all on we'll see if I become a superhero.

Have children help you put on the mask. **What superhero do I look like now? Batman® wears a mask, doesn't he? Why do you think he wears a mask? Without his mask and superhero costume, Batman® would be just an ordinary person like you or me.**

Have children help you put on the cape. **Which superheroes wear capes? Superman® wears a cape, doesn't he? Do you think it helps him fly? Could he be Superman® without it? Why or why not?**

Have children help you put on any other items you've brought. **Wow! Look at me now. I feel like a real superhero. I wonder if I can fly?** Jump up in the air. **Hmm. Nope, guess not. Well, I guess I won't be needing this cape then.** Take off the cape. **And the rest of this superhero gear—I don't think it's going to give me any special powers, do you?** Take off all the superhero gear.

• If I didn't have any of this stuff, could I still be a superhero? Why or why not?

Even without my superhero costume, I'm still powerful. I don't have x-ray vision like Superman®, or nifty bat-gadgets like Batman®. But I have a special power that I can use to do good things and help people just as superheroes do. It's the power of the Holy Spirit. Invite a volunteer to read Acts 1:8 from a Bible.

As followers of Jesus, it's our job to let other people know that Jesus loves them. In our neighborhoods, schools and communities—and all around the world—people need to hear about Jesus. God gives Holy Spirit power so we can do this.

• What words or actions would you use to show Jesus' love?
• How could the Holy Spirit help you do those things?

Spreading the good news about Jesus is a big job. But with Holy Spirit power we can get it done. I'm going to write the initials HS on each person's hand. Holy Spirit power! Write "HS" on each child's hand.

Let's pray. Dear God, thank you for sending the Holy Spirit to give us power. Help us to use the power you give to tell other people about you. In Jesus' name, amen.

Close by having kids hold their fists up in the air as they cheer together, "Holy Spirit power!"

Great Counsel

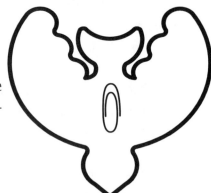

On Your Mark

Bible Truth: We receive power from the Holy Spirit to do God's work.

Bible Verse: But the Father will send the Friend in my name to help you. The Friend is the Holy Spirit. He will teach you all things. He will remind you of everything I have said to you. John 14:26

Godprint: Wonder

Get Set

You'll need a Bible, a magnet, blue poster board and a pen. Before church, use the pattern (right) and cut six to eight doves from construction paper. Tape a small paper clip to the back of each dove.

GO!

Jesus lived on earth for 33 years, then he died on the cross for us and rose again. Then it was time for him to go back to heaven. But before Jesus left earth to go to heaven he promised his disciples that a special helper would come to them. Do you know who that was? Yes, the Holy Spirit!

- Who can tell me something about the Holy Spirit?
- Where does he live? *(Right here! Inside of me.)*
- How much power does he have to help you? *(Lots and lots.)*

The power of the Holy Spirit helps big and little people. He helps them live a life that pleases God. He helps believers to have faith that grows big in Jesus. And the Holy Spirit also helps us live our lives as God's children sharing the Gospel with others.

When Jesus was baptized, the Spirit of God came down to him like a dove. Let's use these little doves to remind us of the Holy Spirit while we think of ways the Holy Spirit can help us today.

Hold up a paper dove for the kids to see. **I'll write an idea on each little dove! Let's see. I can think of one. When I want to talk to my friends about Jesus but I don't know what to say, the Holy Spirit gives me the words. I'll write "words" on this dove.** Pause to write. **And**

sometimes when I pray to God, I don't know what it is I should pray for. The Holy Spirit helps me there, too. I'll write "prayers" on another of my doves.

Encourage the children to come up with more ways the Holy Spirit helps believers. Write as many words on the doves as time allows.

Now let's see if can get these little doves back into the sky where they belong. Hold up the poster board. Try to stick a dove to the board. The dove will fall to the floor. Try again, and again.

Oops! Something's not right. When I try to do things for God all by myself, things don't seem to fly right. I need the Holy Spirit!

Ask two helpers to hold the poster board sky. Hold the magnet behind the poster board and have another child stick a dove to the front. As you move the magnet the "paper-clipped" dove will fly right along! Children may want to try several of the doves.

Now put your hands over your hearts. Ask the congregation to do the same. **God's Holy Spirit lives in the hearts of all believers. He lives in you so the work of the Father can be done through you.**

Let's pray. Holy Spirit, please fill us with your power and love. In the name of Jesus Christ we pray, amen.

What Are You Backpackin'?

On Your Mark

Bible Truth: God gives rest to all who follow him.

Bible Verse: Come to me, all of you who are tired and are carrying heavy loads. I will give you rest. Become my servants and learn from me. I am gentle and free of pride. You will find rest for your souls. Serving me is easy, and my load is light. Matthew 11:28–30

Godprint: Trust

Get Set

You'll need your Bible, a backpack and bricks or rocks. Photocopy and cut apart the labels on page 84, then tape them to the bricks or rocks. Mark Matthew 11:28–30 in your Bible and put it in the bottom of the backpack. Place the bricks or rocks in the pack on top of the Bible.

GO!

Place the backpack a little ways from the children. Struggle to lift the backpack. Stretch your back as you say, **Whew! This thing must weigh a ton! I think I need some help**. Ask a volunteer to move it a little closer. Then choose another volunteer, giving several children a chance to lift the pack and move it a short distance until the backpack is in a spot where all the children can see as you unpack it. Open the pack.

I wonder what's in here that is making it so heavy. Let's see! Remove the rock labeled "lying." **Lying—that means not telling the truth. I lied once to my mother because I didn't want to get in trouble. Have you ever told a lie? Ephesians 4:15 says we are to speak the truth in love if we want to grow in Christ.**

Remove the "worry" rock. **Worry! Wow! That's a heavy one. Sometimes life just seems out of control. I forget that God can handle anything. In Matthew 6, Jesus told his followers not to worry because God knows what we need and he will care for us.**

Remove the "unkind words" rock. **Unkind words. Ouch! Have you ever been hurt by something someone has said to you or about you? Have you ever hurt someone with your words? Proverbs 12:18 says that our words can stab like a sword. But it also says that kind words can heal**. As you remove each rock and read the label, give a personal example or explanation and a Bible verse to ensure that the children understand the action.

After removing all the rocks, lift the backpack. **Wow! Getting rid of all those heavy burdens sure has made this backpack lighter. I think I can carry it now. But what will I do with all these rocks?**

Take your Bible out of the backpack and ask a volunteer to read Matthew 11:28-30.

You know, sometimes we walk around carrying a heavy load because we are holding on to sin or worry or troubles instead of giving them to Jesus. That's not what God wants for us. He wants us to bring all our burdens to him. He has promised to take our heavy load and give us rest.

Let's pray: Thank you, God, for promising to take our heavy burdens so we don't have to carry them. We bring them to you now—our worry, our guilt, our actions and words that hurt others and make you sad. Give us your rest. In Jesus' name, amen.

Lying

Cheating

Guilt

Worry

Selfishness

Unkind Words

Arguing

Disobeying

Tied Up With Dad

On Your Mark

Bible Truth: God ties us to himself with love.

Bible Verse: I led them with kindness and love. I did not lead them with ropes. I lifted the heavy loads from their shoulders. I bent down and fed them. Hosea 11:4

Godprint: Love

Get Set

You'll need a Bible, a paper sack filled with Happy Father's Day ties from years gone by, a hand mirror and a bag of Hershey's Kisses® and Hugs®.

GO!

Who can tell me something that only a dad can do? Listen to responses.

Some things no one else does as well as Dad. For instance, no one can add too much salt to spaghetti or put the wrong color socks on the baby or leave the car windows down in the pouring rain like good ole Dad!

• What makes your dad special?
• How is his love for you like nobody else's?

Of course, Dad can do a lot of things very, very well. Like putting together bikes that come with a gazillion pieces. And how about knowing when, where and how to change a flat tire? But one of the best things that dads do well is knotting ties. Some dads wear ties to keep their shirts looking neat and tidy.

Hold up a tie for the kids to see. Grab a handful of ties from the bag and stand. Turn toward the congregation.

We'll need a few dads to come up and help us make some beautiful ties to wear.

Invite as many dads as you have ties to come up, tie a knot and put the tie around the neck of a child. Pass around the hand mirror so kids can see themselves all beautifully "tied up."

Ties hold shirt collars together. And when the knot is strong it will stay in place a very long time.

Have kids who are not wearing ties check out the knots of the kids with ties. No choking!

God ties us to himself with love. The Old Testament tells us that Israel, God's chosen people, took for granted their special relationship with him. In love he delivered them from Egypt and the suffering of slavery. And while they were in the desert, God walked with them. He fed them and gave them water to drink. God's tie to them was strong. The people didn't always obey God, but he always loved them.

Read Hosea 11:4 from a Bible or ask an older child to read it.

On Father's Day we can be thankful that our Heavenly Father cares for us and leads us with kindness and love. Let's also thank God for our wonderful earthly fathers who give their time and energy to care for us every day. The next time your father puts on a tie and steps out the door, let the tie remind you of his love and God's love.

Distribute the candy "kisses" and "hugs." **When you get back to your seat go and give your dad a great big "Happy Father's Day" kiss and hug! If your dad's not here, give whoever you came with a "hug" and "kiss" of appreciation.**

Let's pray. Thank you, God, for our fathers. Through them we see your love and wonderful care. In Jesus' name, amen.

Olly-Olly Outs in Free

On Your Mark

Bible Truth: Jesus came to set us free from sin.

Bible Verse: Those who belong to Christ Jesus are no longer under God's sentence. I am now controlled by the law of the Holy Spirit. That law gives me life because of what Christ Jesus has done. It has set me free from the law of sin that brings death. Romans 8:1–2

Godprint: Forgiveness

Get Set

You'll need a Bible.

GO!

If we were to play hide and seek right now and you could go anywhere in the church, where would you hide? Don't tell me, because in just a minute I'm going to give you ten seconds to hide. Then I'm going to come looking. After I find the first person, I'm going to call "Olly-olly outs in free" and everyone else can come back without being tagged. Ready? Hide!

Cover your face and count "One, one thousand; two, one thousand..." up to ten.
Find and tag one person, then call "Olly-olly outs in free." Gather the kids around you again. Ask the congregation to send in any stragglers they spot.

Did you know that God went playing hide and seek with Adam? See, it says so right here in the book of Genesis in the Bible. Have a volunteer find and read aloud Genesis 3:8–9 from a Bible.

• Who knows why Adam wanted to hide from God? *(Because he and Eve had disobeyed.)*
• What did God do when Adam hid? *(He called out "Where are you?")*
• Did God know where Adam was? *(Yes. God knows everything.)*
• Then why did God call out? *(To give Adam a chance to come back on his own.)*

God is sad when people hide from him. He loves us so much that he wants to be close to us in our hearts. He wants us to welcome him into everything we think and do. But ever since that first time when Adam and Eve sinned, people have been hiding from God. Of course, God could always find them. But he wanted to make sure everyone got the

message that they could come back freely. That's why he sent Jesus to take our sins to the cross. Jesus took our punishment so God could call out "Olly-olly outs in free!"

Jesus came to earth and showed us what God is like. He helped lots of people and didn't hurt anyone. But when soldiers and priests came to arrest him, he didn't play hide and seek. He let himself be caught. And then he died because of the wrong things you and I have done. And when he rose again, he made a way for us to live forever with him. So when Jesus finished the job he had to do, God could call out to the whole world, "Olly-olly outs in free!" We can come back to God freely without being afraid. All we have to do is trust our lives to Jesus and accept the forgiveness he offers.

Let's pray. Dear Lord, thank you for sending Jesus to take our sins to the cross. Thank you for forgiving us. Thank you that we can live with you forever. Amen.

Be sensitive to kids who are ready to accept Christ and look for an opportunity to follow up.

Pull kids into a huddle and whisper that on your count, they should call out, "Olly-olly outs in free!" as they return to the congregation.

Chocolate Meltdown

On Your Mark

Bible Truth: You can't hide your sins from God.

Bible Verse: Anyone who hides his sins doesn't succeed. But anyone who admits his sins and gives them up finds mercy. Proverbs 28:13

Godprint: Repentance

Get Set

You'll need your Bible, some chocolate chips, and clean wipes or wet paper towels. Before you begin your talk, put your Bible on a table or chair near where you will talk to the children. Hold the unwrapped chocolate clasped in your hands. (Yes, you *want* it to melt and get messy.)

GO!

Try to create an atmosphere of secrecy with your body posture and a stage whisper. As you stand with your hands tightly clasped (chocolate melting) say, **I've got a secret! I'm hiding something in my hands that I don't want anyone to see. Can you guess what I have in my hands?** Encourage the children to make guesses without revealing what you are holding.

I think that if I just keep it hidden, no one will know what it is. I'm just going to keep it tight in my hands and no one will ever know that it's there. Today we're going to look at a Bible verse in Proverbs. Go to your Bible and look puzzled about how to open it without using your hands. Finally, open your hands and reveal the messy, melted chocolate. **I can't open my Bible with these messy hands. Wait a minute while I clean up this mess**. Use the wipes or towels to clean your hands.

- Why was it a bad idea to try to hide those chocolate chips in my hands?
- What would happen if you tried to hide chocolate chips in your hands?

Those chocolate chips melting in my hands remind me of our Bible verse for today. Read Proverbs 28:13 from your Bible.

Trying to hide our sins from God is even more impossible than trying to hide those chocolate chips in my hands. We can't possibly do it.

• Why can't we hide our sins from God?
• What should we do instead of trying to hide our sins? *(Confess, repent.)*

Not only does God know our sins, but often others find out as well. When you do something wrong, the wisest thing to do is to admit what you have done.

• What does our verse tell us happens when we admit our sins? *(Read the verse again if necessary. We find mercy.)*
• What does "mercy" mean?

Mercy means not getting what you deserve. Sin separates us from God. We deserve to be separated from God when we sin. But God showed his mercy when he let Jesus willingly take our punishment for sin. Because Jesus did that for us, we have forgiveness if we believe in him.

Don't try to hide your sin. Admit what you have done and ask God for his forgiveness. God has promised to forgive. If you would like to talk more about being forgiven for your sins, talk with your parents or come see me and we will talk together with you after our time here.

Let's pray. Dear Lord, thank you for showing us mercy. Help us to admit when we do something wrong and not try to hide our sins from you. Please forgive us when we admit our sins and give us mercy. In Jesus' name, amen.

Fresh 'n' Fruity

On Your Mark

Bible Truth: It's sweet to have God's character growing in me.

Bible Verse: But the fruit the Holy Spirit produces is love, joy and peace. It is being patient, kind and good. It is being faithful and gentle and having control of oneself. There is no law against things of that kind. Galatians 5:22–23

Godprint: Discipleship

Get Set

You'll need a bag of wrapped fruit-flavored candies and your Bible. You might want to write the fruit of the Spirit on a poster board, each in a different, bright color. Optional: a bowl of colorful fruit.

GO!

If you have a bowl of fruit, show it to the kids. **Mmmm! I love fresh fruit in the summer time! The only thing I like better than fruit is fruit-flavored candies**.

Unwrap a piece and put it in your mouth, making a big show over how much you are enjoying it. **It's so fresh and fruity and sweet! Would you like a piece?** Pass out a piece of candy to each child. Encourage them to go ahead and indulge—it will help make the lesson "stick."

You know, as sweet and fruity as this candy is to us, the Bible tells us of a fruit that is even sweeter. Read Galatians 5:22–23 or ask a strong reader to help you out.

• Did you catch the names of the fruit God grows in us? How many can you remember? (Pause and give kids time to name as many as they can.)

Love, Joy, Peace, Patient, Kind, Good, Faithful, Gentle, Self-control. Show the poster board if you are using one.

• What do you think love tastes like? (Encourage the children to share their ideas. You might suggest a few words like yummy, sweet, delicious.)
• How about joy or peace?

We can only imagine what these fruits *taste* like, but we know what they look like and feel like, don't we? How would you finish the sentence "Love is…?" Give kids the opportunity to give examples of what love means to them. Emphasize answers that demonstrate the kind of love God wants to develop in each of us.

Now, with your faces, show me what joy looks like. Enjoy the looks of rapture!

Who can tell me what peace is? You may want to call on older volunteers for this response. Respond positively to all answers, emphasizing those that demonstrate godly peace. Then share the following examples for the remaining fruits or ask kids to describe as many of the words as you have time for.

Patient:	waiting quietly when someone else is busy and not nagging; not getting upset or angry when problems come up.
Kind:	being friendly and helpful even to people you don't know and sharing with others.
Good:	telling the truth and obeying without complaining.
Faithful:	being loyal so others know they can trust you.
Gentle:	behaving in a sensitive way, showing that others' feelings are important, too.
Self-control:	accepting responsibility for your own actions and feelings.

The fruit of the Spirit is sweeter than any candy. God has promised to help grow this fruit in our lives. We can help other people know what God is like by how we treat other people—with the fruit of the Spirit. Sometimes God uses other people, like our parents, to help grow these sweet fruits in us. Sometimes we see them grow from hard times or troubles. And sometimes, maybe best of all, they grow in us as we spend more time in God's Word getting to know him and talking with him. I am so thankful that God has promised to grow these sweet fruits in us.

Let's pray. Dear Lord, thank you for giving us your Spirit to help us be more like you. Remind us of the fresh and fruity fruit of the Spirit every day so we can show other people what sweet fruit looks like. In Jesus' name, amen.

The Color Purple

On Your Mark

Bible Truth: God wants us to treat others fairly.
Bible Verse: Stop judging only by what you see. Judge correctly. John 7:24
Godprint: Fairness

Get Set

You'll need a Bible, a picture of a bat (the mammal, not the baseball kind!, poster board and colored markers. Make a poster board sign. Print in large bubble letters the following words: Purple, Green, Blue, Orange, Red and Yellow. Important! Color in each word with a color other than what the word says.

GO!

Keep the sign out of sight for now.

Have you ever seen a pig fly? Pause. **No? What about a cow jump over the moon? Hmm. What about beetle bugs dancing the hokey pokey? In all my years of working with kids, I have had more than a few tell me such things really do happen. After all, they saw it with their own two eyes!**

Well, our eyes only tell part of the story. Hold up the picture of the bat for the kids to see. **For many years, people thought that bats were hideous creatures because of how they looked. Eek! Now we know that bats eat insects and bugs that can drive people and animals itch-crazy. Can you show me how bats fly?** Place your thumbs together and spread out your fingers and "flap."

Good job! Now poke two of your fingers into the air like this. Stick up both pointer fingers. **Let's say you meet a boy or girl on the playground.** Twitch your "people" fingers. **He or she looks nice enough but...**Bend your fingers down to touch your thumbs forming two "wheels"... **the wheelchair he or she is sitting in makes you think twice. You think maybe that boy or girl won't be fun to play with. You quickly walk away.** Have your fingers "walk away." **The Bible tells us not to judge people by how they look. Be fair. Seeing doesn't tell the whole story!**

• What makes a person beautiful on the inside?
• How did Jesus treat the sick and disabled in the Bible?

Hold up the bubble-letter poster and run your finger under each word. **I'd like you to tell me the color you see in each word…not the word itself. Remember, the color, not the word. Ready? Go!** What your kids see—the word—conflicts with what they don't see, the correct color! **Maybe we should get a little help.** Stand and hold the poster up for the congregation to see. **You try it! Tell me the color you see not the color you read…and as quickly as possible. One, two, three!** The congregation will have the mumble jumbles just like the kids!

What you see is not always the whole story. Let's find out what Jesus said about that. Read John 7:24 from a Bible or ask a volunteer to do so.

Jesus was a poor carpenter with no money or power, yet he performed amazing miracles. "Who? He? Couldn't be!" the people shouted. And because they judged him unfairly they gave up the chance to know the true Son of God. So don't judge. Be fair. There is always more to a person than meets the eye. Now…eyes right here!

Put the poster away. **God's way makes sense even if we can't see it right away. Trust him and don't judge others—no matter what your eyes tell you!**

Let's pray. Dear Heavenly Father, help us not to be quick to judge others. Please help us to treat others the way you would treat them. In Jesus' name, amen.

Catch and Release

On Your Mark

Bible Truth: God wants us to offer what we have to him to use in his way.

Bible Verse: [Andrew] said, "Here is a boy with five small loaves of barley bread. He also has two small fish. But how far will that go in such a large crowd? John 6:9

Godprint: Generosity

Get Set

You'll need a Bible, a bag of goldfish crackers—enough that each child has one with some left over in the bag—and one whole, unsliced loaf of bread. Place the items in a lunch box or brown bag. Optional: more bread or rolls to share with the congregation.

GO!

I had to rush out of the house this morning without any breakfast! But I didn't want my stomach growling in church, so I packed a snack. I brought along two kinds. Show the items in your bag. **I have goldfish crackers and my favorite kind of bread for toast. I didn't have time to toast it, but I brought it anyway. I'm pretty hungry. Do you think it would be okay if I ate right now?** If someone says "No," go with it; otherwise say it yourself.

No, that would be rude, because all of you are here and you might be hungry, too. Is anyone hungry? If no one is, say, If you were hungry....

• Since some of you are hungry, what could I do with my goldfish? *(Share them.)*

That's a good idea. I'm hungry and I did want my snack, but I'm willing to share my goldfish with everyone. I'll take one and (pass the bag) **now each of you can take one.** Take a minute for everyone to munch.

Even though I didn't get to eat all the goldfish, I feel good that I shared. And look, there are some left over for later. I think I'll eat my bread next. Take the whole loaf out and get ready to bite into it.

Wait! Maybe some of you are still hungry and would like a bite. But I'm hungry, too. What

should I do? I already shared my goldfish. Do I have to share everything? Should I share (hold loaf out toward the kids), **should I not share** (pull bread in to your chest)? Share (hold out again), **not share** (pull back in)?

I know! Let's see if God says anything about this in the Bible. Open your Bible to John 6:9 and read the verse.

Hey, this sounds similar.

• What did the boy bring with him? *(Five small loaves of bread and two fish.)*
• What was he planning to do with his food? (Eat it.)

That boy had gone out for the day to listen to Jesus teach. He brought a snack because he knew he would get hungry before he got home.

• Was he the only one listening to Jesus? *(No. John 6:10 says there were about 5,000 men plus women and children there.)*
• Probably some other people had food, too. But do you think anyone packed enough to feed everyone? *(No.)*
• Do you think the boy knew what would happen when he gave Jesus his food?

Let's see what happened. Read John 6:11.

• Who did Jesus feed with the boy's snack? *(Everyone who was there.)*
• Did the boy get to eat after all? *(Yes.)*

The boy was willing to give everything he had to Jesus, and Jesus used it to bless lots of people.

Mmm. I still have my loaf of bread. I could keep it to myself and I wouldn't be hungry anymore. Or, I could share it with all of you so you can have a blessing, too! Who wants a piece? Help children tear pieces off.

Optional: If you have enough bread, encourage the children to tear off large pieces or hand out rolls that they can share with others in their families.

Before we enjoy the rest of our snack, let's pray. Dear Lord, thank you for the example of the little boy who shared. We want to share what we have so you can use it to bless other people. Please help us to be generous every day. In Jesus' name, amen.

Pray and Pray S'more

On Your Mark

Bible Truth: Jesus teaches us how God wants us to pray.

Bible Verse: "Father, may your name be honored. May your kingdom come. Give us each day our daily bread. Forgive us our sins, as we also forgive everyone who sins against us. Keep us from falling into sin when we are tempted. Luke 11:2–4

Godprint: Prayerfulness

Get Set

Place the following items in a paper sack: a party invitation, chocolate-covered graham crackers, marshmallows, sticks, a flashlight and a red balloon with the blowing end cut off. You'll also need a Bible.

GO!

Open your Bible to Luke 11:2–4 and hold it in your lap.

- Who taught you how to pray?
- Who do you think taught Mom or Dad?

Jesus was a teacher—a very good teacher. And do you know why? Because he taught by example. One day his disciples saw him praying in his special place. They waited patiently for him to finish and then one of them asked, "Can you show us how to do that?" Or in other words, "Teach us how to pray, please." So Jesus stopped what he was doing and gathered his disciples around him. Then he said: "When you pray, this is what you should say."

Father...
Reach into the bag and pass around the invitation. **God *invites* us to believe that he is our true Father and we are his children.**

May your name be honored...
God wants us to set his name apart. That means to keep it clean, pure and bright in our hearts. Stretch the red balloon over the flashlight lens. Turn on the flashlight and place it on the floor in front of you. **We'll use this to remind us to keep God bright in our hearts.**

May your kingdom come...
The Holy Spirit helps us be part of God's kingdom here on earth. Arrange the sticks "campfire style" on top of the flashlight. **The sticks will help us think of the earth, and we'll pile them right over God's light.**

Give us each day our daily bread...
Jesus' words here mean food plus all the other things our body needs. Hand each child two chocolate-covered graham crackers. **No nibbling just yet!**

Forgive us our sins, as we also forgive everyone who sins against us...
We pray that God our Father would not look at our sins but see us bright white and brand new, just like these marshmallows. Then we forgive the mistakes other people make, too. Hand each child a fresh, white marshmallow straight from the bag. **No eating yet!**

Keep us from falling into sin when we are tempted...
We pray that God would keep us safe from the devil and from things that tempt us to do bad things. Put your marshmallow between your graham crackers. I know you've been tempted to eat your goodies from the start. I now give you permission to go ahead and take a bite!

Rub your hands over the crackling fire! **The campfire is really warming my hands! You know, when I place a marshmallow between graham crackers** (make a S'more of your own!) **and take a bite I feel as if I'm camping in the woods on a chilly night with the big, beautiful moon shining above. The next time you go camping and the fire is warm and toasty and out come the chocolate bars, marshmallows and graham crackers, remember the Lord's Prayer! Jesus taught his disciples how to pray. And he teaches us, too. Pray and pray S'more!**

Let's pray. Ask the congregation to join you in repeating the Lord's Prayer.

Buy One, Get One Free

Bible Truth: Jesus wants us to give freely to others.
Bible Verse: You have received freely, so give freely. Matthew 10:8
Godprint: Generosity

Get Set

You'll need a Bible and a stack of store coupons. Make sure you have a "buy one, get one free" coupon in your stack. If you cannot find one, make one.

GO!

• What's your favorite thing about going food shopping?
• When your family goes shopping, who's in charge of the store coupons?

After the service today I'd like to head to the beach (or park) **and have a picnic. So I have some shopping to do.** Thumb through the coupons you have in your hand. **Let's see, I have to get ice, soda, fruit, a bag of chips and some sandwiches.** Allow a few coupons to spill to the floor. **Oh, no! My coupons are really out of hand! Who'd like to help me?** Distribute the coupons among the kids.

• Does anyone have a "buy one, get one free" coupon?

I really look for these coupons in the newspaper. All I have to do is buy one thing and I'll get the second thing free. Sounds good, doesn't it? Pause. **But you know, if I have to buy something I don't really need, it's really not all** *that* **free, is it? What kind of coupon would beat a "buy one, get one free" coupon?** Have kids try to guess.

You're close. What about a "buy nothing, get everything free" coupon? Then all I'd have to do is walk into the store and say to the clerk, "I'd like to take you up on this 'buy nothing, get everything free' coupon!"

• What things do we get from people who love us that cost no money?

Jesus is the best kind of super-saver. He saves big! If he were passing out coupons, the only one he'd give is the free, free, free kind. The very best kind, indeed. We wouldn't have to bargain or barter or give him any money. And the free gift he offers each of us is better than any Christmas or birthday gift. Really!

• What great gift does Jesus give us that is "absolutely free?"

Read from a Bible the last phrase of Matthew 10:8: "You have received freely, so give freely."

Jesus asks us to freely give to others as he has freely given to us. Being generous and offering friends lemonade on a hot day is a wonderful "free" thing!

• What has God given to you freely?
• How can you freely give to others?
• How do you serve Jesus when you give to others?

Remember, everything we have is a gift from God to freely share with others.

Let's pray. Thank you, Jesus, for giving to us so freely. Thank you for your free salvation. We will give to others freely too. Amen.

Ask your kids to stand and turn toward the congregation. Now before you return to your seats, find someone out there to give your coupon to. Hand it off and say, " Jesus gave freely, and so can you!" Then return to your seat. Go!

Growing Up

On Your Mark

Bible Truth: God wants us to grow to be more like Jesus.

Bible Verse: Instead, we will speak the truth in love. We will grow up into Christ in every way. Ephesians 4:15

Godprint: Discipleship

Get Set

You'll need a Bible, a bunch of grapes, scissors, a ball of green yarn and a large cardboard cross. Cut a six-inch length of yarn for each child. Reserve the rest of the yarn.

GO!

Do you know anything about growing plants? I want to grow a certain plant, and I've had nothing but trouble. I know I need to start with a seed, but then what do I do?

Give each child a piece of green yarn. **Let's roll up our yarn and pretend it's a seed. Make a fist with one hand and poke your "seed" down into it. Okay, we've now planted our seeds in the dirt. Now what? Water? Okay, let's water our seeds.**

Pretend to water the seeds, then show children how to pull their yarn up so it's showing just above their fists. **Great! My plant is starting to grow. Maybe I'll have better luck this time.** Pull a little more yarn out of your fist. Keep pulling the yarn until it falls over. **See—that's my problem. I can't get my plant to stand up and grow.**

- Is it okay for the plant to grow on the ground? Why or why not?
- What might happen to a plant growing on the ground?

Some plants are supposed to grow on the ground. Pumpkins and zucchini grow on the ground. They grow long vines with big leaves and big flowers and big vegetables so they'll get noticed and not stepped on. Potatoes and carrots grow under the ground. It doesn't matter if we step on their leaves, because their vegetables are safe underground. Plants like beans and peas don't do well on the ground. They have thin, curly vines and small leaves and vegetables that aren't as noticeable. But beans and peas aren't my problem.

My problem is bigger. My problem is heavier. My problem is grapes. Hold up the bunch of grapes. Then hold up your yarn. **Do you think this little vine could hold up this bunch of grapes? Probably not. And if the grapes sit on the ground they'll eventually rot and be no good to eat. I need to figure out a way to keep the grapevine from falling over. Any ideas?**

Grapes and other viney plants need to be supported as they grow. They need to be trained to grow *up* a lattice or trellis so they don't fall *down* on the ground. The Bible says that's kind of like our life with Jesus. Have a volunteer read Ephesians 4:15 from a Bible.

We need to support each other as we grow in our faith so we can all grow up toward Jesus. Let's see how our little grapevine might do with a little support.

Help children form a human lattice. Have one row of children kneel and link elbows. Have a second row stand behind them and link elbows. Have one child stand behind the second row and hold the cross up high.

Look at this good, strong lattice. As I wind the vine around your arms, tell us one way you can help a friend grow to be more like Jesus.

Wind the yarn around the children. When you've finished, tie the grapes to the end of the yarn. **Look! Our grapes aren't falling over! When we help each other, we can all grow up to be more like Jesus.**

Let's pray. Dear God, you are the gardener who knows how to make us grow. Help us to grow and be more like Jesus. Make us into strong vines that serve you. In Jesus' name, amen.

Heavy Metal Music

On Your Mark

Bible Truth: God wants us to praise him so our leaders can know him.

Bible Verse: Kings, hear this! Rulers, listen! I will sing to the Lord. I will sing. I will make music to the Lord. He is the God of Israel. Judges 5:3

Godprint: Praise

Get Set

String together a metal cheese grater, a metal sieve, a metal colander and a small metal pot. Also bring along one kitchen ladle and three metal spoons. Place everything in a paper sack. You'll also need a Bible.

GO!

Keep the paper sack with the stringed kitchen gadgets close by. **Good morning, music lovers! Do I have a brave volunteer to sing a few bars of a favorite patriotic song?** Pause. If no one volunteers, hum a few bars and see if the children will join you.

A lot of us feel shy about singing, especially in front of other people. What if the mayor of our city asked you to sing? Who is the leader of our country? Would you sing in front of this person?

• If you could choose any song to sing for our leaders, what would you choose?
• What if you didn't want to sing, but you could make music another way? What would you do?

The Old Testament has a story about two people who sang a song in front of their leaders. The story is about Deborah and Barak. They sang about how God had helped his people and how powerful God is. Let's read some of the words of their song.

Open your Bible to Judges 5:3 and hand it to a reader to read the verse aloud.

• Who did Deborah and Barak call out to in this song? *(Kings, rulers.)*
• We may not have a king, but who are our rulers or leaders?
• What did Deborah and Barak sing about for the leaders? *(The Lord.)*

Wow! Let me hear a few joyful shouts to the Lord right now. Pause. **How about we have the congregation join us?** Have your kids turn to the congregation. **On the count of three, let's all give a joyful shout to our loving Lord. One…two…two and a half…three!** You're bound to get a puny little shout from the congregation at first. Shake your head. Have your kids shake their heads too! Then ask kids to cup their hands to their ears and shout, "We can't hear yooooou!" Pause to allow the congregation to redeem themselves. **My goodness! That *is* a whole lot of joy!**

Return your attention to the kids. **Deborah and Barak said they would sing to the Lord, but they also said they would make music to the Lord. They wanted their rulers to know they were praising God. Let's make a little joyful music of our own right now to celebrate God and the wonderful country we live in!**

I'll need a conductor. Put your hand in the paper bag and take out the ladle "baton." Hand it to an enthusiastic volunteer. **I also need three musicians to stand close to me and hold these percussion sticks.** Distribute the three spoons. **I'd like everyone else to be the rhythm chorus. Watch and do what I do.** Demonstrate the following actions for the children. **Slap your knees twice like this. Then clap your hands twice. And finally snap your fingers twice. You can pretend to snap even if your fingers won't work right.** Practice the rhythm with your kids until they can feel the beat. **I think we're ready to make some joyful music unto the Lord!**

Conductor, please wave your baton to get us started. Chorus, please perform your rhythm beat. Pause while everyone gets the beat going. Then reach into the bag and pull out the string of "musical instruments." Nod to your "spoon" musicians. **Please tap out a lovely melody on my string of "heavy metal" instruments! From our hands to his ears we'll play with joy to please our awesome God!** Give a signal for the conductor to stop.

I hope this week you'll remember to praise God and not be afraid if anyone hears you.

Let's pray. God, it gives us great pleasure to play our praises to you. Help us to be thankful for the country we live in and to help others in our country know we praise you. Amen.

Dough-too! Dough-not!

On Your Mark

Bible Truth: God knows best and wants us to obey him.

Bible Verse: I have not come down from heaven to do what I want to do. I have come to do what the One who sent me wants me to do. John 6:38

Godprint: Obedience

Get Set

You'll need one doughnut (with a hole!), a box of doughnut holes, an "Albert Einstein" wig (wispy, messy and white), and signs that say, "Doughnut Lovers Unite!"

GO!

Do we have any food experts here? Choose a child and ask him or her to stand. Place the wig on top of the child's head. **Ah, yes! All experts have hair just like this. Did you know that bad hair proves how smart you really are! Just ask Einstein!**

Here we go. Food Expert #1: Who is Dr. Pepper® and how did he get his name on a can of soda? Listen to the inventive answer.

I didn't know that! Wonderful! Now who would like to be our Food Expert #2? Have the first child hand the wig to the second child.

Food Expert #2: Why do dead fish stare up from the plate when you eat them?

Pause, listen to the giggles, and then hold up the doughnut (with the hole) for your kids to see. **Now for the hardest question yet. Do I have one last food expert in the group?** Adjust the wig on your last volunteer. **Food Expert #3: I just love a cup of hot apple cider and a delicious doughnut. But I have one question: Why do doughnuts have holes in the middle?**

After the child responds, place the wig on your own head and stomp your foot. **It's not fair. I want a whole doughnut with nothing missing in the middle and I want it now!** Pass out your protest posters and invite your kids to stage a peaceful protest march around the congregation with you in the lead!

Put the posters away and sit back down. The Bible tells us we can't always get what we want. And that's the way it should be! Listen to what Jesus tells us in the Bible in John 6:38. Read the verse from a Bible.

• Who is "the One" that Jesus talks about in this verse?
• Why should you follow Jesus' example and do what God wants you to do?
• What do you think God wants you to do for him?

For Jesus, obeying his Father's will meant dying on a cross so that we could be saved. God will let you know what his plan is for your life. Read the Bible. Then pray and obey! Eternal life with Jesus awaits all those who obey the will of his Father. Heaven! That's better than a hundred doughnuts!

Hold up the whole doughnut again.

• What do you think a doughnut with no hole would be like? Would I really want one?

Doughnuts have holes for a very good reason. Without the hole, doughnuts would be crusty fried lumps with lots of uncooked dough inside. I only thought I wanted a doughnut with no hole. But that's not really the best for me.

Here, have a doughnut hole while you think about it! Offer the doughnut holes to your kids. **Remember, obey God and do what he wants you to do. God knows best.**

Let's pray. Dear God, we want to obey you the way that Jesus did. Help us to do what you want us to do. In Jesus' name, amen.

Up, Up and Away

On Your Mark

Bible Truth: God can do amazing things in our lives that we can't even imagine.

Bible Verse: God is able to do far more than we could ever ask for or imagine. He does everything by his power that is working in us. Give him glory in the church and in Christ Jesus. Give him glory through all time and for ever and ever. Amen. Ephesians 3:20-21.

Godprint: Confidence

Get Set

You'll need two balloons inflated with air, each tied to a long string, and two balloons inflated with helium also tied to long strings. Prepare the balloons to be quickly and easily attached to the children's wrists by tying a slip-knot at the end of each string. Recruit a couple of grown-up or teenage balloon-tying assistants. You'll also need a Bible.

GO!

Keep the balloons out of sight as you begin.

It's a great day to celebrate God's love and power! That's what coming to church is all about—celebrating God! So in a way, church is like a party. One of my favorite things about parties is balloons. I brought some balloons to our church party today. I also like to play games at parties. Today we're going to play a game with balloons.

• Which of you thinks you can keep a balloon in the air above your head without holding it?

Choose four kids to participate in the game. Carefully, so that kids will not realize that some balloons contain helium, attach balloons to the children's wrists. You may need some grown-up helpers for this— one person to firmly hold the balloon while the other ties it on. **You must hold it with both hands until I say, "Go." Then let go of the balloon and keep it above your head without holding on to it. You can touch it, but you can't hold it.**

When I say, "Go," keep your balloons up until I say, "Stop." Ready? Go! The kids will quickly realize that some balloons have helium while others do not. After a few seconds, stop the game and collect the balloons.

Let's give three cheers for our balloon bouncers!

• Some people had more trouble keeping their balloons up. Why was that?

Two had to do it all by themselves, but the others had some help from a little helium. Sometimes, as we try to do what God asks us to do, we think we have to do it all by ourselves without any help from him. But the only way we can really do what God wants is with his power working in us.

Sometimes it's hard to follow God, especially when we put our confidence in ourselves. Let's listen to Ephesians 3:20-21. That's in the New Testament. It's part of a letter that Paul wrote to a church family a lot like ours. Read Ephesians 3:20-21 from a Bible or ask a volunteer to do it.

• What do these verses say that God does for us? *(More than we ask; works in us by his power.)*
• How does that make us more confident in the work we do for God?
• What should we do in response to what God does for us? *(Give him glory.)*

Wow! God does more than we can ask or imagine! Some of you have really good imaginations! But these verses remind us that God is bigger than anything we can ask for or even imagine. The things we can do for God don't depend on how smart, pretty, strong or talented we are. When we put our confidence in the things that we can do, we are a lot like our balloon bouncers who just had air in their balloons. They were sure working hard, but that balloon kept coming right back down.

With God's power working in us, we are more like the ones with helium balloons. Hold one of the helium balloons by the string. **Just like the helium keeps this balloon floating in the air, God working through us can allow us to do things we can't even imagine. You can put your confidence in that!**

Let's pray. God, you are so powerful—more than we could ever imagine. Thank you that you use your power to work in us. We give you all the glory for everything you do. In Jesus' name, amen.

Optional: After the service, as the children leave, pass out helium balloons to each to remind them of the lesson.

Index of Topics and Godprints

Index of Scripture Passages